# THE BIG-FLAVOR GRILL

# THE BIG-FLAVOR GRILL

## NO-MARINADE, NO-HASSLE RECIPES FOR DELICIOUS STEAKS, CHICKEN, RIBS, CHOPS, VEGETABLES, SHRIMP, AND FISH

**Chris Schlesinger & John Willoughby**

Photography by Ed Anderson

**TEN SPEED PRESS**
Berkeley

# contents

# introduction

**LATELY, IT SEEMS,** cooking has become very complicated. Brine this. Marinate that. Make a sauce that takes three days. It seems like you have to take a week off to throw a dinner party.

We want to dial it back, to get out from under the yoke of complex formulations and intricate preparations. We want to take you back out to the grill, where cooking can be spontaneous and the food is easy but full of bold, intense flavors. One of the very best things about grilling is that it is a supremely simple process.

Or at least it should be simple. Because when you get down to it, all you really need is a fire, a grid, and a few bricks to hold up that grid. So when we go out to the grill, we want to cut through the scores of gadgets, the humongous gas burners, five different smokers, grapevine cuttings, all of the trappings that have been foisted onto grilling over the past couple of decades, and get back to easy creation of big flavors. Sorry, guys, about all your gadgets and secret sauces. We believe grilling is about proper technique and the flavors that are created through that technique. Fancy equipment and complicated strategies are just distractions.

In addition to being simple, grilling should be easy. So in the pages of this book, we hope to remind those of you who already know, and show those who don't, that big flavor does not need to be the result of big effort.

We learned this ourselves not from going to culinary school or practicing the techniques of classic Euro-style cooking, but from traveling in the tropics. If you want delicate, nuanced shadings of flavor in your food, then the labor-intensive creations of classic European cuisines are probably for you. But if you're looking for deep, explosive flavor without much work, then the hot-weather regions of the world are the placec to look.

Why? Because these two parts of the world have very different approaches to the process of developing flavor in a dish.

Much Euro-derived cooking employs what we like to call an "architectural model," in which a range of individual flavors are combined to create a single new taste. To make a classic French sauce, for example, you first spend hours roasting bones and then cooking down water with those bones in it to create a base stock. Then you reduce this further with aromatics and maybe some meat. Then you reduce it further with herbs. Then when you're almost done, you slowly blend in a ton of butter. The result of all this is a kind of taste pyramid, with the top of the pyramid being a single, well-blended, subtle, intricate articulation of flavor.

But do you really want to do all this? Maybe once in a while, in the dead of winter when spending all day by the stove seems like a good idea.

But here's the other option: a Latin salsa. Chop up some perfectly ripe tomatoes, add some chiles and onions and a good dose of cumin, squeeze in a couple of limes, sprinkle in chopped cilantro, and you're good to go. What you get is a dish with what we call a "geographical model," in which one flavor after another—sour, sweet, bitter, hot, aromatic, earthy—is laid out for your taste buds in rapid succession. Rather than the long, smooth ride on a single flavor, you get the jolt and hum of many tastes. When properly done, each flavor complements and underscores the others, but they are all perfectly distinct.

To us, this geographical model is an equally valid approach to cooking. And to us, the big, bold, contrasting, competing but complementary flavors of hot-weather food are the more exciting option.

It's no coincidence that the standard method of cooking in hot climates, even to this day, is grilling over live fire. And grilling (assuming you're using charcoal or some variety of wood as your fuel) adds another element of smoky, seared flavor to anything you cook. So by its very nature, it mediates against any attempt to introduce subtlety or blended flavors.

In addition, this is also the part of the world where spices originated. This means that even everyday cooks in these regions are experts in spice use, and the intense flavors of these dried seeds, roots, barks, pods, and shoots are inextricably integrated into the cuisines.

Not coincidentally, grilling and spices are a very good combination. One of our favorite ways of using spices is to whip up a spice rub—a mixture of spices based on one of scores of traditional combinations from around the word—then coat the food with the rub before it goes over the fire. We long ago adopted spice rubs in place of marinades, the more traditional option for flavoring grilled foods. We did so because we found that spice rubs have all kinds of advantages over marinades. Since rubs consist almost solely of spices, at most moistened to a paste with a bit of oil, they provide stronger, better-defined flavors than marinades. They also stick better to the surface of foods, which again intensifies the flavor. Plus you can put them on at the last minute instead of having to think ahead, as you do with a marinade—and to us, not having to think ahead is definitely a major advantage.

But even with all their virtues, spice rubs aren't the be-all and end-all of big-flavor cookery. If we used only them, we'd miss the other flavors that you can get with marinades: the spark of citrus; the heavy, gentling sweetness of hoisin; the funk of fish sauce; the fresh licorice taste of basil; the familiar burn of fresh chiles. Since these ingredients don't really lend themselves to spice rubs, we began to think about how to bring them to our grilled dishes—and came up with what we like to call "razzle-dazzles."

This concept was actually developed down in Costa Rica. Along with a group of friends, we are part-owners of a little house on the water down there, and one of the primary activities is cooking. Everybody does a little something—someone makes the salad, someone grills the entrée, someone mixes the cocktails, someone figures out snacks for those predinner drinks. But the selection of ingredients down there can be limited. So we buy shrimp at the market when we can, or buy fish from a fisherman, or sometimes just go with the super-thin pork chops from the local bodega.

Whatever we find, we're not looking to do anything fancy with it. Without a full kitchen—and with the ocean temptingly close—we don't want to spend lots of time on dinner. But we do want to put some real flavor on it.

So folks started to make what we came to call razzle-dazzles, easy combinations of ingredients that you could toss together with already-grilled food to add bold flavors. We're talking about the handful of fresh-chopped herbs, the squeeze of lemon, the plunk of hoisin and fish sauce, the dollop of chile-garlic sauce—in other words, the simply made, fresh, quick, easy addition *after* grilling.

In addition to its ease and the bold flavors it contributes, the razzle-dazzle approach makes it easy for a group of folks to cook together. Our friend Ihsan might volunteer to build the fire, and Chris would say, "I'll do the grilling. Who's going to make the razzle-dazzle?" Everybody gets to participate without feeling burdened, not to mention that creating razzle-dazzles is an excellent way to let your creativity and sense of flavor flower without a lot of overhead.

To us, razzle-dazzle is the next step, after spice rubs, in replacing marinades. Because when you marinate something, you take lots of ingredients, spend time chopping them and mixing them, put the main ingredient into it, and let it sit until the flavors are melded. Then, you toss out the marinade and grill the meat—which all too often tastes like it's been soaked in Italian dressing. Think how different it is to simply grill the main item, put it in a bowl, then one by one add all the ingredients you would have used for a marinade and give it all a good toss. You experience each ingredient in its full-on, distinctive glory as opposed to having all of them soaked and discarded together.

This is important because, when you use the "big-flavor" approach to cooking, you need to use several flavors at the same time. Sweet without hot, sour without aromatic, or earthy without bitter is not that interesting. And when you combine all the ingredients, as you do in a marinade, they lose their punch and their distinctness.

So our preferred approach is to grill the main item, put it in a really big stainless steel bowl, then add all the remaining ingredients individually, and toss vigorously to combine them. The act of tossing itself is important here, too. Of course you can mix gently with a spoon or a pair of tongs (or your hands), but we like to actually toss, in the kind of rolling flip that chefs use to toss food in a sauté pan over a burner's flames. It's the best way to mix everything up without crushing anything, plus it's got a bit of showpersonship to it, which somehow always makes the food taste a little better to your guests. It looks fun, and it's *à la minute*, which is chef-speak for made to order.

But the most important point to remember is that this is casual food. This is not food for trying to impress anyone. This is everyday food you want to eat. If your friends like it, too, that's good. But even that is not essential. All that's imperative is that you like it, and that you have fun cooking it. We think you will.

Oh, and for those of you who like a bit more challenge with your cooking, each recipe chapter includes a "Curve Ball." This is a dish that involves a little more advance preparation, requires slightly more intricate technique, or in some other way deviates from the ease inherent in our usual grill-and-toss approach. It's still in the ballpark, but it curves just outside the parameters of simplicity we usually adhere to. Knock yourselves out.

Although grilling is a simple and straightforward cooking technique, that doesn't mean there are no rules. So we're going to lay out for you here our understanding of the principles of grilling. We think that taking a glance at them will make cooking over live fire even easier and more enjoyable for you. At least we hope so. Because, after all, it's only after you really understand something that you can feel fully at ease with it.

# WHAT IS GRILLING?

Grilling is the act of cooking food directly over the heat from a live fire. It's just that straightforward. In fact, grilling is probably the first method used by humans to cook their food, and has remained unchanged in its essential nature since that time. That's one of the reasons why we love it.

But grilling is also much more than that. For today's griller, perhaps its cardinal principle is that it's fun.

For one thing, grilling is the most interactive form of cooking. Unlike a stove or oven where you just turn a dial, when you're grilling you actually create your source of heat as you build your fire. And, since no two live fires are exactly the same, you are likely to keep fiddling with the fire as cooking progresses. So grilling is the most involving way to cook, an entertainment in and of itself.

Paradoxically, it's also the most relaxed and easygoing of cooking methods. At least in this country, grilling has always been associated with casual get-togethers, informal gatherings—the kind of easy backyard camaraderie that virtually defines the American character. It's hard to be stuffy or formal when you're all gathered outside around an open fire enjoying a couple of beverages while someone cooks dinner. So by its very nature, grilling tends to be at once celebratory, low-key, and happy. It's no wonder it has become so insanely popular over the past couple of decades.

Yet grilling is also a bona fide cooking method that was defined, along with other techniques such as roasting and braising by the preeminent nineteenth-century French chef, author, and culinary codifier Escoffier. Sometimes grilling tends to be thought of as a lesser cooking technique, merely the province of inexperienced backyard cooks and therefore worthy of less respect. Not so, scoffers. Grilling has serious cred.

So how would grilling be defined in those terms? Well, it might help to think of it as similar to sautéing, another method of cooking directly over high heat, but with the added benefit of the smoky char that comes from live fire. When food is exposed to the direct heat of the flames, a seared crust develops on its exterior, and it is this flavor-packed crust—rather than the fuel used for the fire, as many believe—that is most responsible for the characteristic grilled flavor. The flavor that the sear provides is created by a process that most of us just call browning, but that is known to scientists and aficionados as the "Maillard reaction." To put it simply, this reaction occurs when carbohydrates and proteins are heated together. When this happens, the sugar (from the carbohydrate) and amino acids (from the proteins) combine to form new chemical structures. As heat continues to be applied, these compounds in turn break down, producing literally hundreds of by-products, each of which has a distinctive taste and aroma. What does all this mean? Your food gains a whole bunch of new, rich, deep, complex, kick-ass flavors.

But there's also a third characteristic of grilling that adds even more to its appeal: it's an incredibly versatile cooking method that pairs naturally with bold flavors. If you think grilling is just for hamburgers, hot dogs, and the occasional steak, think again. There are an enormous number of people in the warm weather world who rely on grilling as their everyday cooking method. For them, cooking over live fire is not a weekend ritual, and it's not a highly defined professional technique: it's just the way they cook.

This means that looking to this part of the world will yield an enormous number of ideas from which to choose your inspiration when you light the grilling fire. Watching someone grilling a mess of shrimp on a beach in the Yucatán, eating skewers of grilled lamb in a Moroccan bazaar or grilled beef in a market in Saigon, or sitting down to platters of grilled peppers, tomatoes, and eggplant in Istanbul, you realize that the range of possibilities for high-flavor grilled food is virtually endless.

So there you have it, our three perspectives on grilling: the easy, casual, have-a-blast approach that Americans bring to the cookout; the technical understanding of practiced chefs; and the international range of flavors and foods grilled by the cooks of the hot-weather world. When these three approaches come together, you've got it all: interesting new flavors, easy cooking, and a lot of fun along the way.

But before we go out to the grill, let's run through some things you should know.

# TOOLS, FUELS, AND FIRE

First let's talk about the tools you need, the fuel you should use, and how you should deal with laying and lighting your fire.

## Tools:
### You Don't Need Most of Them

Every year there are more grilling gadgets on the market. Some of them (like the little lamps that clamp onto the side of the grill so you can see what you're doing at night) are actually pretty useful. Most of them, however, are just attempts by manufacturers to get you to part with your money. In the spirit of simplicity that this book is all about, we are giving you the bare basics here. If you have these, you're ready to grill; whether you buy more toys and tools to play with while you're standing over the coals, we leave up to you.

### A Grill

There are all kinds of charcoal grills on the market, from clunky to stylish, giant to balcony sized, basic to tricked out. We believe that, as long as your technique is right, you can do a perfectly good job of grilling by using an oven rack suspended above the ground by a couple of piles of bricks, so we don't offer a whole lot of advice about which grill you should buy. However, there are a few things to keep in mind: (1) For maximum versatility, buy the biggest grill you have room for and can afford. You can always grill just a single chicken breast on a giant grill if you want, but it's hard to fit a whole brisket or a pork butt on a smaller grill. (2) Get a covered grill. This allows you to smoke-roast and to do hot smoking, both of which are excellent techniques that you can't do if you end up with a noncovered grill. (3) All things being equal, it's best to have a grill grid that has those little flip-up areas that allow you to add fuel to the fire without taking all the food off the grid.

### Tongs

Tongs are perhaps the second most important piece of grilling equipment, after the grill itself. They act like a pair of hands that can't be burned, and we use them for everything from putting food on and taking it off the grill to rearranging the charcoal to lifting up the grill grid when we need to add more fuel. We recommend that you get at least two or three pairs so they're always within reach. Just be sure that you get sturdy tongs that are spring-loaded so they open and close without your having to manipulate them. It's also good to have at least one pair of long-handled tongs, which makes it easier to work above a hot fire without burning yourself.

### A Cleaning Brush

Having a clean grill grid is important not just to avoid "off" flavors imparted by previous grilling sessions, but also to get a better sear on meat and to keep fish from sticking. The easiest way to keep your grid clean is to brush it thoroughly when you're finished grilling; the bits of food that get stuck to it come off more easily when still hot. There are all kinds of brushes made specifically for this, and most of them work well enough. But if you want to save a little cash, go to the hardware store and buy one of those wire brushes designed to remove paint. It works just as well, and it's cheaper than most grill-specific versions. This is particularly good because in our experience none of these brushes lasts more than one season anyway.

## A Chimney Starter

This is the best way to start your charcoal fire. Extraordinarily simple in design—a metal cylinder with a handle, a grid a couple of inches up from the bottom, and some holes around the sides—it works every time with virtually no effort. Just put some newspaper in the bottom, fill the rest of the cylinder with charcoal, and light the paper. In about fifteen minutes, your charcoal will be well enough lit to dump out into the grill. Other than the covered grill itself, this might be the best grilling invention of the twentieth century. We recommend you get the large one, since you can always put less charcoal in if you want a smaller fire.

## The Fuel

We are fans of hardwood charcoal. Although it used to be pretty hard to find when we first started recommending it, it's now readily available. The advantage of this type of fuel is that it's pure carbon, produced by burning wood in the near-total absence of oxygen. As a result, it lights more easily and burns hotter and cleaner than charcoal briquettes, which are basically compressed sawdust mixed with binders. That said, you can grill perfectly well over briquettes, so if that's what's available—or that's just what appeals to you because it's what your father grilled over—go ahead and use them. And by the way, if you have access to hardwood logs, here's a little trick we like to use: Take a small log and lay it alongside the charcoal

once it's well started. It will add some smoke flavor to whatever you're cooking, plus it burns more slowly than the charcoal, so you have a longer-lasting fire. Just use whatever hardwood is most readily available wherever you live, but be aware that if that happens to be mesquite, you're going to add a very distinctive flavor to your food.

## The Fire

This is the heart of the matter. Most of the fun and challenge of live-fire cookery has to do (not surprisingly) with the fire itself. Knowing how to set it up the right way will ensure that you have the options to react effectively to the way each individual piece of food is cooking; knowing how to light it will have a profound effect on how much of a pain you think the process is.

## Laying the Fire

There are basically two ways to lay your charcoal fire. First, you can distribute the coals more or less evenly over the entire bottom of the grill, which gives you the same level of heat wherever you put the food. Or you can put all the coals on one portion of the grill and leave another portion with no coals. The latter type of fire is known, logically enough, as a two-level fire. The usual recommendation is that you build a single-level fire when you are cooking something like steak, which spends its entire time directly over the coals, and build a two-level fire only when you are cooking something that you sear over the coals and then move to the area with no coals to finish cooking at a lower heat. But we recommend that you *always* make a two-level fire. It's no more work, and even if you are planning to cook your food right over the coals the whole time, you never know—fires are unpredictable, and it might turn out that one of your steaks cooks faster than the others and needs to be moved off the coals to finish up. Even more importantly, having an area with no coals allows you to deal with flare-ups in the proper manner. What this means is that when a flare-up occurs, you simply move the offending piece of food to the coal-free area until the flames die down. So it just makes sense to leave about half to a third of the grill free of coals when you lay your fire.

## Starting the Fire

When it comes to starting a charcoal fire, nothing is easier or more reliable than the chimney starter. All you do is set it in the middle of the fire grate, fill the bottom section with crumpled newspaper, then fill the top with charcoal and light the newspaper. The flames will sweep up through the chimney, igniting the charcoal. When the charcoal is red hot, dump it out and, if you want more charcoal, just dump it on top of the portion that's already lit. Of course, the chimney is not the only option. Despite its bad reputation, we think lighter fluid is just fine. If you wait until the coals are all lit before you start cooking, which you should do in any case, the fluid will all be burned off long before you put anything over the fire, so it won't affect the taste of the food. (Just be sure to avoid "quick-lite" charcoal, which is fully impregnated with chemicals, so it will release them onto your food the whole time you're cooking.) Whichever fire-starting method you use, it will take about half an hour for the fire to work up to the fiery-red stage and then die down until all the coals are covered with a fine, gray ash, at which point you can start checking the temperature of the fire to see if it's ready for you to cook.

## A WORD ABOUT GAS GRILLS

Though you can't argue with their convenience, gas grills are not really our thing; we prefer the interactive excitement of cooking over live fire, where every cooking experience is slightly different. Well, truth be told, Chris takes an attitude on this, but Doc, as John is known, has been known to use a gas grill during the week, because it's just quicker and easier. So don't pay any attention to the high-attitude chef; just do what you want. In any case, you can certainly make all of the recipes in this book using any gas grill. Each step in getting ready to grill is, of course, quicker. First, instead of waiting for the coals to come to the right temperature, turn all the burners to high, close the lid, and let the grill preheat for fifteen minutes. At that point, if the recipe calls for a two-level fire, instead of banking the coals on one side, all you have to do is turn off half the burners. And instead of holding your hand above the grill grid to judge the fire's temperature, simply turn the dial to the proper setting. But one thing you should be aware of: unless you have a super-powerful big-ass gas grill (and even if you do), the heat from gas can never equal the heat from coals—it's just in the nature of the beast. So you may need to add an extra minute or two of cooking time to anything that one of our recipes instructs you to cook directly over a hot charcoal fire.

# PROCESSES, OR THINGS YOU NEED TO KNOW AND DO

So let's say you've bought all the essentials, and you're ready to lay and light your fire. Here are some other principles of grilling that you should pay attention to before you begin. They're not really rules, just principles that will make you a better griller.

## Get Your *Mise en Place*, or Be Prepared

Whether you prefer the French culinary phrase or the Boy Scout motto, having everything ready and close at hand before you start to grill is critical to success. As soon as you've lit the fire, get to work preparing all your individual ingredients. We like to put them in stainless steel bowls, but any appropriately sized containers, from coffee cups to clean small yogurt containers to muffin tins, will do. Set up a table by your grill and lay out all the ingredients, preferably in the order you're going to use them. Then make sure you have whatever tools you will need for the grilling task at hand; get any platters or bowls you will need for putting food on when it comes off the grill; check to be sure you have a good supply of your favorite beverage; and put on your game face. Grilling is easy, but it's often fast and requires some concentration, so you don't want to be distracted by having to run back into the kitchen for something you've forgotten. Besides, if you've ever cooked with a professional chef, you know that a hallmark of their professionalism is that they are completely set up before they take the first step in cooking anything. It makes everything after that much easier and more relaxing—not to mention that standing out by the grill with everything all laid out and ready to go makes for a very dramatic moment. As the griller, you are going to look very cool, unassailable in your steady calm and steely resolve.

## Know the Fire Temp

Since not all foods are best cooked over the same heat, it is important that you check the fire's temperature before you put anything on the grill. The good part is that, though it is somewhat inexact, it's easy to do. Just allow the flames to build up and subside, and then, when the coals are uniformly gray, put your hand about five inches above the grill grid: if you can hold it there for only two or three seconds (go ahead and count it out: one-one-thousand, two-one-thousand . . .) you have a hot fire; three to four seconds is a medium-hot fire; four to five seconds is in the medium range; and five to six seconds means you have a low fire.

## Be Ready to Deal with Flare-Ups

Flare-ups are an inevitable side effect of grilling anything that has fat in it. And they're not really that terrible—most of them die out quickly and aren't going to adversely affect the flavor of the food. But major flare-ups can deposit soot on the food, so you need to be prepared to deal with them. If you've followed our advice and built a two-level fire (see above), you're ready: simply move the food that's above the flare to the cool area of the grill and wait for the flames to die down. It's that easy. One thing you should *not* do, though, is follow the advice you'll find in many grilling books and magazine articles and use a water squirter to put out flare-ups. When you do this, you are likely to create a plume of ash that gets all over your food, which is obviously not a good thing.

## Avoid Cover-Ups

Our general rule of thumb about using the grill cover is this: unless something is on the grill for forty-five minutes or more, don't use that cover. And here's the reason: if you use the cover for those relatively short-cooking items, your food has a tendency to come off the grill with a kind of "off" flavor. Somewhat difficult to describe, this flavor—slightly ashy and a bit metallic, with a kind of soggy smokiness—is nevertheless readily recognizable to any practiced griller. Our three-quarters of an hour rule is admittedly somewhat arbitrary. But to our taste buds, that is approximately how long it takes for the smoke flavor created during covered grilling to become more prominent than the "covered" flavor. So for these short-cooking items, if you should need to create an "oven" effect, cover the food with a disposal aluminum roasting pan or pie plate. And here's a corollary rule: when you're smoke-roasting, which is to say cooking something for a relatively long period of time with the grill cover on, don't put the food directly over the coals. If you do, the fat dripping into the coals will sometimes impart a similar, off flavor to the food. So build your two-level fire, as always, and put the food that you're smoke-roasting over the part of the grill with no coals.

## Is It Done Yet? Know How to Tell

The ability to know when your food is properly done may be the single most important skill of a successful griller. In addition to a thermometer, which we don't use often, there are two ways of checking your food for doneness.

### The Hand Method

The hand method rests on a basic scientific principle: as proteins cook, they become firmer. Because of this, professional cooks can judge the degree of doneness of a piece of meat simply by pushing on it with a finger and assessing its firmness. (It's called the "hand method" because, to make it easier to teach young cooks, chefs have come up with a system of comparing the texture of food at various degrees of doneness to the texture of the base of your thumb when you're touching the thumb with each of the four fingers.) The only problem with this method is that it requires a lot of experience to use with any degree of accuracy. So by all means practice poking your food while it's cooking to judge its doneness, and over time you'll gain expertise and confidence. But for your basic, standby, everyday way of checking doneness, we recommend the old tried and true "nick, peek, and cheat" method.

### Nick, Peek, and Cheat

As the name implies, you simply pick up one of whatever you are cooking, nick it slightly with a knife so you can look inside, and check its state of doneness. That's all there is to it. You couldn't get much easier or more accurate. Unfortunately, many home cooks fear that cutting into a piece of meat lets all the juices out, a fear that is encouraged by many grilling "experts." But the thing is, it's not true. Yes, a drop or two of juice may escape when you nick the food, but that's it. And that very minor loss of juices pales in comparison to serving raw or burned food. This method truly does not harm the food, and we urge you to make it your friend. Just remember that carryover cooking will boost the food a little further toward doneness. So take that steak off when it looks rare if you really want it medium rare, for example, and remove the fish from the flames when it has just a tiny trace of transparency in the middle, since your ultimate aim is a fish that is just translucent in the center.

## Use Lots of Salt and Pepper

The ability to properly use salt and pepper is another of the handful of skills that separate a good cook from a great one. Most cooks don't use enough salt. And as for pepper, it is the spicy underpinning of all Western cooking, and should be treated as such. So when our recipes say to "sprinkle generously with salt and pepper," we mean exactly that. Be more generous with these two old standbys than you think you should be, and you'll likely find your cooking notably improved. In fact, Chris highly recommends that, at least one time, you purposely overseason something. Keep adding salt until that steak or chop or piece of fish or whatever it is you're cooking has become too salty for you. It will probably take a lot more than you think to get to that point, and it will also be a valuable yardstick for the future, so you not only know how the taste of the food changes as you add salt, but you'll also know how far is too far for you.

We like kosher salt because it generally has fewer additives than table salt, but primarily because its large crystals make it easier to judge just how much you're adding when you use your fingers, which is the best and most fun way to do it. (By the way, because of its large crystals, the same volume of kosher salt has only half the amount of salt by weight that table salt has; so if you're using table salt, cut any of our actual salt measurements in half.)

As for pepper, there is no comparison between fresh-ground and preground; it is definitely worth the small amount of extra effort, and in fact is a critical component of almost every one of our recipes. We like to grind our peppercorns coarsely so the little chunks explode with flavor and heat in your mouth when you bite into them. For the coarsest grind, crack the peppercorns by rolling a heavy sauté pan back and forth over them while bearing down on the pan. For a somewhat finer texture, just use the coarser setting of your pepper grinder.

## And Once More: Say No to Marinades

We know that we're coming down a little hard on the "no marinating" business. The reason is that, at least in this country, marinating has always been closely associated with grilling. This seems to derive from the idea that marinating not only adds flavor and moisture that will stay with the food through the rigors of the grilling process, but that the process also tenderizes the food. Neither of these is really true. Marinades don't penetrate very far into meats or other proteins, so the flavor they add is pretty much only on the surface. And while acidic marinades will tenderize foods somewhat, they really only tenderize the surface—and in fact they just make that surface slightly mushy. Add this to the fact that marinades are more work than spice rubs or razzle-dazzles, require advance planning, and meld flavors rather than leaving them individual, bright, and distinct, and we think there are a lot of good reasons to avoid marinades.

And now . . . enough talking. Let's get to the recipes.

STEAK

# skirt STEAKS

**WE LIKE PRETTY MUCH ALL STEAKS**, but the skirt steak is our #1 favorite. One of the three so-called "flat steaks"—along with flank and hanger—this long, thin, flat steak is kind of the embodiment of the principle that, when it comes to beef, there is an inverse relationship between tenderness and flavor. Like its flat brethren, the skirt does not come from the short loin or sirloin, which are the luxe, tender parts of the cow. Instead, it comes from the area between the abdomen and chest cavity, where the muscles get more exercise and so are tougher. What that translates to is a steak with a ton of rich, deep, beefy flavor. That's true of the other two flat steaks, too, but the skirt has the advantage of having considerably more fat than the others, which means it is richer and juicier and has even more intense, meatier flavor. All of this is what's good about skirt steak. The bad part—the one drawback—is that over the past decade or so, as more and more chefs and home cooks have recognized its virtues, it has gone from dirt cheap and readily available to relatively expensive and somewhat hard to find. Actually, this trend started when fajitas became popular, because they were originally made from skirt steak, which back then was a thrifty choice. Even now, though, it is cheaper than the more tender steaks, because Americans seem to value tenderness above flavor in their meat. So our advice is to keep your eyes open when you go to the grocery store, and whenever you see some skirt steaks, snatch them up—and always choose the fattiest ones, which have the best flavor. Skirt steaks are also very easy to grill, requiring nothing more than eight to twelve minutes above a hot fire, which will give the outsides a nice, strong sear before the interior overcooks. In fact, we are such big fans of the flavorful crust on skirt steak that we put a spice rub, which intensifies that crust, on even the simplest recipe. Since it's a very basic rub, it also works in all the other recipes here. One final word of caution: don't overcook these babies, because they get tough if you take them above medium rare. Also, when they come off the grill and have rested a bit to reabsorb their juices, be sure to slice them thinly on the bias against the grain. This is another way to make them tenderer, since slicing them this way cuts through the muscle fibers, and shorter fibers are less tough.

# Super-Basic
# GRILLED SKIRT STEAKS

20

# Super-Basic
# GRILLED SKIRT STEAKS

2¹/₂ pounds skirt steak, cut into 4 to 6 pieces

1 tablespoon ground cumin

1 tablespoon paprika

1 tablespoon coriander

2 tablespoons freshly cracked black pepper

Kosher salt to taste

¹/₄ cup olive oil

 Build a two-level fire in your grill, which means you put all the coals on one side of the grill and leave the other side free of coals. When the flames have died down, all the coals are covered with gray ash, and the temperature is hot (you can hold your hand 6 inches above the grill for only 2 to 3 seconds), you're ready to cook.

 In a small bowl, combine the spices and salt to taste and mix well. Rub the steaks all over with the oil and then with the rub, pressing gently to be sure it adheres.

Serves 4 to 6

Put the steaks on the grill directly over the coals, and cook until done to your liking, about 4 to 6 minutes per side for medium rare. To check for doneness, cut into the thickest steak and peek to see if the meat is slightly less done than you want it to be when you eat it.

 Transfer the steaks to a cutting board, tent them loosely with foil, and let them rest for 5 minutes or so. To serve, slice the steaks thinly on the bias against the grain.

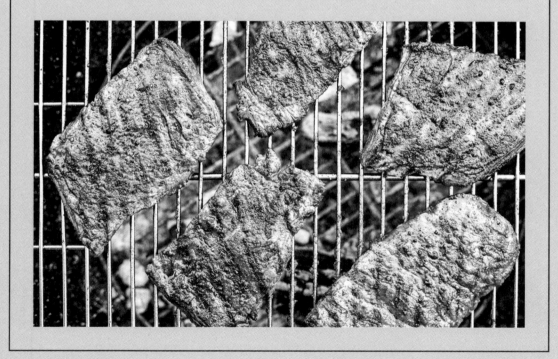

# GRILLED SKIRT STEAKS with
# STEAK SAUCE-CHILE BUTTER

GRILL UP some thick slices of bread (you can call it Texas toast) and serve the steak on top of it so the bread soaks up the juices and some of the butter.

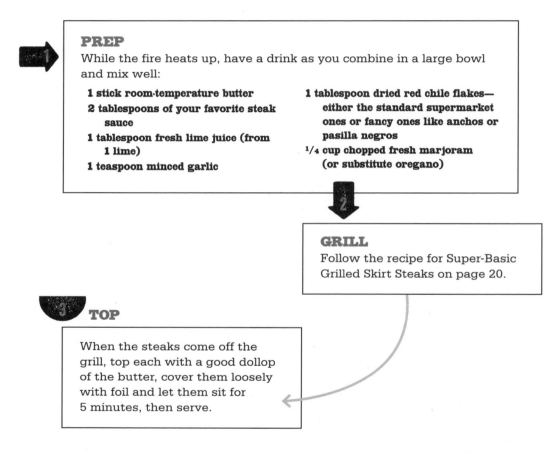

**PREP**

While the fire heats up, have a drink as you combine in a large bowl and mix well:

1 stick room-temperature butter

2 tablespoons of your favorite steak sauce

1 tablespoon fresh lime juice (from 1 lime)

1 teaspoon minced garlic

1 tablespoon dried red chile flakes— either the standard supermarket ones or fancy ones like anchos or pasilla negros

1/4 cup chopped fresh marjoram (or substitute oregano)

**GRILL**

Follow the recipe for Super-Basic Grilled Skirt Steaks on page 20.

**TOP**

When the steaks come off the grill, top each with a good dollop of the butter, cover them loosely with foil and let them sit for 5 minutes, then serve.

# GRILLED SKIRT STEAKS with HONEY-MUSTARD RANCH DRESSING

*THIS IS GOOD served on a bed of arugula for a great, super-flavorful steak salad.*

### PREP
While the fire heats up, combine in a large bowl and mix well:

- 1/2 cup buttermilk
- 1/2 cup mayonnaise (homemade if you feel like it, page 232)
- 1 tablespoon honey
- 2 tablespoons spicy brown mustard
- 1 teaspoon minced garlic
- 1 tablespoon roughly chopped fresh dill

- 2 teaspoons fresh oregano, or 1 teaspoon dried
- 3 shots Tabasco, or more to taste
- Kosher salt and freshly cracked black pepper to taste

### GRILL
Follow the recipe for Super-Basic Grilled Skirt Steaks on page 20.

### TOP

When the steaks come off the grill and have had their rest, put them on a platter and swipe each with some of the Honey-Mustard Ranch Dressing, then pass the rest as a dipping or drizzling sauce.

# GRILLED SKIRT STEAKS with BACON-MUSHROOM RELISH

*THIS IS MORE your classic steak with bacon and mushrooms rather than steak with a relish—but people seem to feel better about eating it when called a relish, so that's what we're naming it.*

### PREP

As the fire comes up to heat, combine in a large bowl, mix well, and set aside:

**¹/₂ pound bacon, cooked and crumbled**
**3 tablespoons extra-virgin olive oil**
**3 tablespoons balsamic vinegar**
**1 teaspoon sugar**
**1 teaspoon ground cumin**
**¹/₄ cup chopped fresh parsley**
**Kosher salt and freshly cracked black pepper to taste**

Combine in a medium bowl and toss to coat:

**1 pound white mushrooms, cleaned and stems slightly trimmed**
**¹/₄ cup olive oil**
**Kosher salt and freshly cracked black pepper to taste**

### GRILL

Put the mushrooms on the grill directly over the coals and move around with your tongs until they're golden and heated through but still firm, 3 to 5 minutes. Remove the mushrooms from the grill and cut into quarters, then add them to the large bowl with the bacon mixture and toss to combine. Now grill the steaks, following the recipe for Super-Basic Grilled Skirt Steaks on page 20.

 TOP

When the steaks are rested and ready to eat, top each one with a good portion of the Bacon-Mushroom Relish, then pass any remaining relish separately.

# GRILLED SKIRT STEAKS with BARBECUED BREAD SALAD

*THIS IS OUR Texas-inspired reinterpretation of panzanella salad.*

## PREP
While the fire heats up, combine in a large bowl and toss well:

**1 baguette, lightly toasted and cut lengthwise into medium dice (about 6 cups, but no need to be precise about it)**
**¹/₂ cup your favorite barbecue sauce**
**²/₃ cup extra-virgin olive oil**
**²/₃ cup balsamic vinegar**
**2 tablespoons roughly chopped garlic**
**3 teaspoons dried red pepper flakes**
**1 cup roughly chopped parsley**
**Kosher salt and freshly cracked black pepper to taste**

## GRILL
Follow the recipe for Super-Basic Grilled Skirt Steaks on page 20.

 ## TOSS

When the steaks come off the grill and have rested, slice them on the bias against the grain. Pour the juice into the bread salad, then put the bread salad onto a platter or individual plates and top with the sliced steak.

# GRILLED SKIRT STEAKS with SMOKY RED ONIONS and GRILLED AVOCADOS

*ONIONS are much easier to grill if you keep them in thick circles—and if you've never had grilled avocados, we predict that you're going to be very happy with them.*

## PREP

While the fire heats up, combine in a large bowl, mix well, and set aside:

- 1/4 cup fresh lime juice (from 2 limes)
- 1/4 cup extra-virgin olive oil
- 1/4 cup fresh orange juice (from 1 orange)
- 2 tablespoons minced chipotle peppers in adobo
- 1 teaspoon minced garlic
- 1/4 cup roughly chopped fresh oregano
- Kosher salt and freshly cracked black pepper to taste

Now prep the avocados and onions.

- 1 large red onion, peeled and cut into 1/2-inch circles
- 2 ripe but still firm avocados, halved and pitted but left in the skin

Rub the onions and avocados with:

- 3 tablespoons olive oil

And then sprinkle them generously with:

- Kosher salt and freshly cracked black pepper to taste

## GRILL

Put the onions on the grill on the side away from the coals and cook until golden brown, about 10 minutes per side. Remove them from the grill, chop them roughly, and add them to the bowl with the prep ingredients.

Grill the avocados face down on the side of the grill until golden brown, about 5 to 7 minutes. Take them off the grill, spoon out or dice the flesh, add to the bowl with the other prep ingredients, and toss.

Now follow the recipe for Super-Basic Grilled Skirt Steaks on page 20.

## TOP

When the steaks come off the grill and have rested, slice them on the bias against the grain, put them on a platter, and top them with the red onions and avocados.

# steak
# TIPS

**STEAK TIPS** are one of our favorite things to grill. In fact, Chris used to think about opening a restaurant that served nothing but tips. So it was surprising to us to find, a few years ago, that lots of people outside of New England don't even know what steak tips are. If any of you are among the deprived who have never eaten them, here's what they are: big cubes of (usually) some type of sirloin steak that are put over the fire until they are nicely crusty on the outside and still tender inside. What's the particular appeal? First, in common with other items we are inordinately fond of, like chicken wings, steak tips have a lot of surface area that can take on a flavorful char over the fire. Second, since they are made from beef that is a bit on the chewy side, these guys have rich, deep, robust beef flavor. And there's actually a third virtue: they are relatively inexpensive. People use various cuts of beef for steak tips, but our #1 choice is a cut called "flap meat." This comes from the bottom sirloin butt (which, by the way, is also the source of the chef's darling known as the tri-tip). In New England, this is a no-brainer, because flap meat is usually sold as "sirloin tips." But in other regions, it may be sold either as "flap steak" or "faux hanger steak," the latter because it bears a physical resemblance to the hanger. Whatever it's called, we recommend you buy it in steak form and cut it into cubes, which gives you more control over the size. Even if you cut them yourself, though, you'll probably end up with cubes of varying thickness, so your cooking time may vary slightly from cube to cube. In any case, we prefer cubes of about two inches, which is the ideal size for maintaining that outer-char/inner-tenderness dichotomy. Also, since they're large enough not to fall through the grill grid, at this size they are easier to grill individually rather than on a skewer, as many cooks do. We like our tips really well browned on all sides, and that's a lot easier to accomplish when they're not skewered. You'll be kept busy moving the tips around with your tongs when they're on the grill, but the results are going to be well worth it.

# Super-Basic GRILLED STEAK TIPS
## 33

### with **Tex-Mex Vinaigrette**
34

### with **Horseradish, Mustard, and Your Favorite Steak Sauce**
35

### with **Homemade Korean Barbecue Sauce**
36

### with **Thai Basil, Ginger, and Lemongrass**
38

### **Five-Spice Grilled Steak Tips** with **Grilled Pineapple** and **Sweet-Sour Sauce**
39

# Super-Basic
# GRILLED STEAK TIPS

2 pounds sirloin steak tips (we recommend tips made
from flap steak), cut into 2-inch chunks

¼ cup olive oil

Kosher salt and freshly cracked black pepper to taste

 Build a two-level fire in your grill, which means you put all the coals on one side of the grill and leave the other side free of coals. When the flames have died down, all the coals are covered with gray ash, and the temperature is medium-hot (you can hold your hand 6 inches above the coals for 3 to 4 seconds), you're ready to cook.

 Put the steak tips in a bowl with the olive oil, salt, and pepper and mix until the tips are evenly coated.

 Put the tips on the grill directly over the coals and cook, rolling them around frequently so they get well browned on all sides, until done to your liking, about 8 to 10 minutes for medium rare. To check for doneness, cut into one of the chunks and see if it's done just a bit less than the way you like it. (Remember that it will continue to cook after being taken off the heat.) Remove the steak tips from the grill, cover them with foil, and allow them to rest for 5 minutes before serving.

| Serves 4 to 6 |

# GRILLED STEAK TIPS with TEX-MEX VINAIGRETTE

*HEAT UP some tortillas on the grill, make yourself a big bowl of guacamole, and your summer dinner is ready to go.*

**PREP**

While the fire heats up, combine in a large bowl and mix well:

- 1/2 cup extra-virgin olive oil
- 1/4 cup white vinegar
- 2 tablespoons fresh lime juice (from 1 lime)
- 1 teaspoon minced garlic
- 1 tablespoon minced red or green fresh chiles of your choice
- 1/4 cup roughly chopped fresh cilantro
- 1 teaspoon ground cumin
- 1 teaspoon ground coriander
- 1 teaspoon chili powder
- Kosher salt and freshly cracked black pepper to taste

**GRILL**

Follow the recipe for Super-Basic Grilled Steak Tips on page 33.

 **TOSS**

When the steak tips come off the grill, put them into the bowl with the vinaigrette and toss, toss, toss—you want them all evenly covered.

# GRILLED STEAK TIPS with HORSERADISH, MUSTARD, and YOUR FAVORITE STEAK SAUCE

OUR PERSONAL top three steak sauce contenders are Heinz 57, A.1., and Worcestershire. Pick one of those, or substitute your own favorite, and try this out.

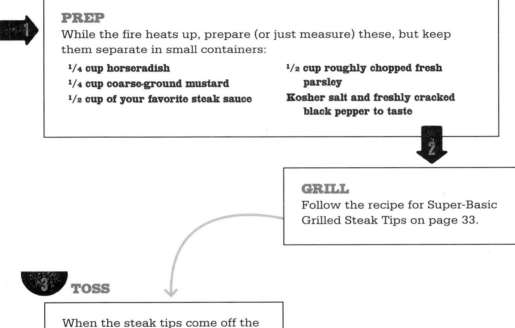

**1**

### PREP
While the fire heats up, prepare (or just measure) these, but keep them separate in small containers:

1/4 cup horseradish

1/4 cup coarse-ground mustard

1/2 cup of your favorite steak sauce

1/2 cup roughly chopped fresh parsley

Kosher salt and freshly cracked black pepper to taste

**2**

### GRILL
Follow the recipe for Super-Basic Grilled Steak Tips on page 33.

**3** TOSS

When the steak tips come off the grill, put them into a very large bowl, then add each of the other ingredients one after the other and toss with style and grace.

# GRILLED STEAK TIPS with HOMEMADE KOREAN BARBECUE SAUCE

CHECK OUT your local Asian store, and you'll likely find prepared ingredients that you're not familiar with but which can quickly and easily add a ton of flavor to your food. The fermented red pepper paste known as gochujang, essential to many Korean dishes, is a perfect example.

## PREP

While the fire heats up, combine in a small saucepan over low heat and cook, stirring frequently, for about 12 minutes—you just want it heated up and well combined:

- 1/2 cup gochujang (Korean fermented red pepper paste)
- 1/4 cup hoisin sauce
- 1/4 cup soy sauce
- 1/4 cup rice wine vinegar
- 2 tablespoons minced fresh ginger
- 2 teaspoons minced fresh garlic
- 1 tablespoon orange zest

Now take it off the heat and let cool to room temperature.

## GRILL

Follow the recipe for Super-Basic Grilled Steak Tips on page 33.

## 3 TOSS

When the steak tips come off the grill, put them into a large bowl, add the barbecue sauce, and toss well.

Toss together in a bowl and then sprinkle the steak tips with:

- 1/2 cup thinly sliced scallions, white and light green parts
- 3 tablespoons toasted sesame seeds
- 1 tablespoon dried red pepper flakes

# GRILLED STEAK TIPS with THAI BASIL, GINGER, and LEMONGRASS

*HERE'S A CLASSIC Southeast Asian combination of superaromatic ingredients. Once again, you'll see that they maintain their freshness and individual flavors best when combined just before the dish is served.*

**PREP**

While the fire heats up, prepare and have ready in small individual containers:

- **1 cup roughly chopped Thai or Mediterranean basil leaves**
- **2 tablespoons minced fresh ginger**
- **1 teaspoon minced garlic**
- **1 to 2 tablespoons chopped fresh red or green chile of your choice**
- **2 tablespoons minced fresh lemongrass, using inner core from bottom one-third of stalk**

- **1 tablespoon toasted sesame oil**
- **¼ cup fish sauce**
- **¼ cup fresh lime juice (from 2 limes)**
- **1 tablespoon brown sugar**
- **Kosher salt and freshly cracked black pepper to taste**

**GRILL**

Follow the recipe for Super-Basic Grilled Steak Tips on page 33.

 **TOSS**

When the steak tips come off the grill, put them into a giant bowl, then dump in the other ingredients one after another and toss with panache.

# FIVE-SPICE GRILLED STEAK TIPS with GRILLED PINEAPPLE and SWEET-SOUR SAUCE

*SURE, TRADER VIC'S is a relic, but it introduced many of us to a certain style of Asian flavor combinations. Here they are in an updated and fresher version.*

### PREP

While the fire heats up, combine the sauce ingredients in a large bowl and mix well:

**1/2 cup ketchup**
**1/3 cup cider vinegar**
**1/4 cup brown sugar**
**1/4 cup soy sauce**

### GRILL

When the fire is ready, put on the grill right above the coals:

**4 (1-inch-thick) slices fresh pineapple, peeled and cored**

Grill the pineapple slices until golden brown, 3 to 4 minutes per side. Remove from the grill, cut into bite-size pieces, and put into a big bowl. Next, combine the following and mix gently:

**3 tablespoons chopped fresh ginger**
**1/4 cup soy sauce**
**1 tablespoon five-spice powder**

Now follow the recipe for Super-Basic Grilled Steak Tips (see page 33), coating the steak tips just before they go on the grill with this five-spice mixture. Then, 45 seconds before the steak tips come off of the grill, brush them with a little of the sauce.

 ### TOSS

When the steak tips come off the grill, put them into the bowl with the pineapple, add the remaining sauce, and toss adroitly. Just before you serve, sprinkle the tips with:

**1/2 cup finely chopped fresh cilantro**

LAMB

# lamb CHOPS

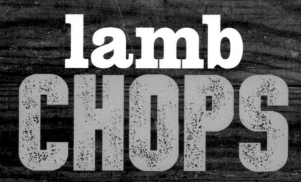

**WE FIRMLY BELIEVE THAT LAMB** is the single most underappreciated ingredient in modern American cooking. This lack of popularity has its roots in our country's history. Beef was considered more luxurious and therefore desirable because in Europe few countries had enough pastureland to raise much beef. Because of this, it was mostly a province of the rich. As a corollary, lamb was thought of as the food of poor people and therefore to be avoided by diners of refinement. But it's high time to get over those old prejudices and start enjoying the many virtues of lamb. In particular, lamb chops on the grill are one of life's great little luxuries. They've got that delicious lamb taste, along with just enough fat to get crisped up by the fire and amplify that flavor. Plus they're tender and kind of delicate for meat, in both terms of size and taste. We're not talking shoulder chops here, which are delicious if cooked right but have a lot of fat and connective tissue, which makes them kind of a no-go for many people. We're talking, instead, about the chops that come from the loin. But there are several types of loin chops. The blade, which comes from the fatty shoulder end of the loin, is still a little too fatty and tough. That leaves us with the rib chop, which is very tender and consists of a single muscle (it is the lamb equivalent of the Delmonico steak), as well as two center-cut chops. The one most often designated simply as "loin chop" is the one that resembles a miniature T-bone, containing a small piece of the ultratender tenderloin muscle and a large piece of the top loin muscle, divided by a T-shaped bone. These are the most expensive chops, but they are also the most tender and have the most subtle lamb flavor, so they are the favorite of many cooks. Top loin chops, which don't have the tenderloin portion, are also excellent in all of these recipes. In fact, any of these three is a fine choice, as long as you buy them bone-in and make sure they are about an inch and a half thick so that they have a chance to get well seared before the interior overcooks.

# Super-Basic
# GRILLED LAMB CHOPS

43

with **Homemade Mint Sauce**

46

with **Feta** and **Sun-Dried Tomato Relish**

47

with **Roasted Red Pepper Relish**

48

with **Roasted Garlic Vinaigrette**

49

with **Smoky Eggplant Blatjang**

50

# Super-Basic
# GRILLED LAMB CHOPS

8 loin or rib lamb chops, each about 6 ounces and 1¹/₂ inches thick

3 tablespoons olive oil

Kosher salt and freshly cracked black pepper to taste

 Build a two-level fire in your grill, which means you put all the coals on one side of the grill and leave the other side free of coals. When the flames have died down, all the coals are covered with gray ash, and the temperature measured above the coals is hot (you can hold your hand 6 inches above the grill for only 2 to 3 seconds), you're ready to cook.

 Rub the chops with the olive oil, sprinkle them generously with the salt and pepper, and place them on the grill directly over the coals. Sear them well, about 3 minutes per side. Now move the chops to the cooler side of the grill and cook, turning once, until the desired doneness (about 4 minutes total for medium rare, which is how we like them). To check for doneness, make a small cut into the thickest part of a chop and peek inside; it should be slightly less done than you like it, since it will continue to cook after it's removed from the grill.

 Remove the chops from the grill, cover loosely with foil, and let rest for 5 minutes before serving.

| Serves 4 |

# GRILLED LAMB CHOPS with HOMEMADE MINT SAUCE

*HERE'S A HOMEMADE VERSION of the ubiquitous green mint jelly of our youth, with the addition of sweet apricot. Could it be any easier?*

**PREP**

While the fire heats up, put in a small sauce pan over medium heat and heat, stirring frequently, until the preserves have become liquid, about 4 minutes:

**1 cup apricot preserves**

Remove the melted preserves from the heat and set aside to cool for 20 minutes. When cool, stir in:

**½ cup finely chopped fresh mint**

**GRILL**

Follow the recipe for Super-Basic Grilled Lamb Chops on page 45.

**3 TOP**

When the lamp chops have finished resting, brush them generously with your homemade mint jelly and serve.

# GRILLED LAMB CHOPS with
# FETA and SUN-DRIED TOMATO RELISH

*IT'S ALL GREEK (flavors) to us. We're usually fans of using local products, but if you can find imported feta, it's much tastier than the domestic version.*

**PREP**
While the fire heats up, combine in a medium bowl and toss gently (you don't want the feta to completely fall apart):

1/2 cup roughly crumbled feta

1/3 cup sun-dried tomatoes, diced small

1/3 cup extra-virgin olive oil

2 tablespoons roughly chopped fresh oregano

Kosher salt and freshly cracked black pepper to taste

**GRILL**
Follow the directions for Super-Basic Grilled Lamb Chops on page 45.

**TOP**

When the chops are rested and ready to serve, top each with a tablespoon or two of the relish and serve.

# GRILLED LAMB CHOPS with ROASTED RED PEPPER RELISH

DON'T WORRY about using jarred peppers here, but if you have the time, make your own: it's fun to burn something to cinders on purpose, instead of by mistake. Check out the recipe on page 233.

## PREP
While the fire heats up, combine in a medium bowl and toss:

³/₄ cup roasted red peppers, jarred or homemade, diced small

1 teaspoon minced garlic

¹/₄ cup roughly chopped fresh basil

¹/₄ cup extra-virgin olive oil

¹/₄ cup balsamic vinegar

Kosher salt and freshly cracked black pepper to taste

## GRILL
Follow the recipe for Super-Basic Grilled Lamb Chops on page 45.

## TOP
When the chops are finished with their rest, top each with several tablespoons of the relish and serve, then pass the rest of the relish separately.

# GRILLED LAMB CHOPS with
# ROASTED GARLIC VINAIGRETTE

*ROASTED GARLIC seems like one of those things you should always have around— might as well do two or three heads while you've got the oven on. And don't forget to zest the lemon before you squeeze it.*

**PRE-PREP**

This recipe has an ingredient you need to make in advance: roasted garlic. Here's how to make it:

Preheat your oven to 400°F (or, better yet, do this when you have the oven going for something else). Slice off the top 1/4-inch from a head of garlic, then put the head in the center of a foot-long piece of foil and pour 3 tablespoons of olive oil over it. Now wrap it up tightly and roast until the individual cloves are soft to the touch, about an hour. To use, separate the head of garlic into cloves and squeeze out the meat.

Now you're ready for the recipe.

**PREP**

As the fire heats up, combine in a medium bowl and toss with enough force to combine well:

**Meat from 1 whole head roasted garlic**
**1/4 cup pine nuts, toasted in a dry skillet over medium heat, shaking frequently, for 5 minutes**
**1 tablespoon lemon zest (from 1 lemon)**
**3 tablespoons fresh lemon juice (from the same lemon)**
**1/2 cup extra-virgin olive oil**
**1/4 cup roughly chopped fresh parsley**
**Kosher salt and freshly cracked black pepper to taste**

**GRILL**

Follow the recipe for Super-Basic Grilled Lamb Chops on page 45.

**TOP**

When the chops are rested and ready to serve, top each with several tablespoons of the roasted garlic vinaigrette and serve, passing the rest of the vinaigrette separately.

*Curve Ball #2*

# GRILLED LAMB CHOPS with SMOKY EGGPLANT BLATJANG

*OKAY, so a blatjang is just the South African name for a chutney. But isn't it more fun to say? Plus, it's good to pay homage to the extensive grilling culture of that country. This blatjang, by the way, is one of Doc's favorite recipes—he's even been known to serve it mixed with brown rice as an awesome vegetarian entrée.*

**1**

## PREP
While the fire heats up, gather together these ingredients:

**3 tablespoons molasses**
**¹/₃ cup red wine vinegar**
**¹/₄ cup roughly chopped fresh cilantro**

**1 tablespoon minced fresh ginger**
**1 tablespoon curry powder**
**Kosher salt and freshly cracked black pepper to taste**

**2**

## GRILL
When the fire is ready but before you put on the chops, put on the grill just around the edges of the coals:

**1 medium eggplant, cut into planks about 1 inch thick, planks coated lightly with olive oil**

Grill the eggplant until well browned and moist all the way through, 5 to 6 minutes per side, then remove from the grill, dice medium, and put in a large bowl.

Now follow the recipe for Super-Basic Grilled Lamb Chops on page 45. But before you put the chops on the grill, coat them, pressing to be sure they adhere, with:

**3 tablespoons crushed coriander seeds**

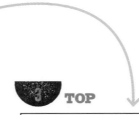

**3 TOP**

While the chops rest, add all of the other prepped ingredients to the bowl with the eggplant and toss furiously. Top each chop with a tablespoon or two of the chutney and serve, passing any remaining chutney separately.

# lamb KEBABS

**KEBABS—OR SKEWERS,** as they are more ecumenically called—since "kebab" is a bastardized form of *sis kebabi,* the Turkish term for meat grilled on skewers—have a long and illustrious history in those parts of the world where live-fire cookery predominates. There are plenty of good reasons for this. For one thing, by cutting meat into cubes you can cook it much more quickly, which means you use less fuel. For another, it's supremely adaptable: as long as you choose something that doesn't need long, slow cooking to become tender, there's really no limit to what you can thread onto skewers and set over the glowing coals. We particularly like lamb skewers, since lamb is the meat of choice throughout the eastern Mediterranean and northern Africa, one of the hot-weather regions of the world where grilling is most common and the flavors are the most exciting.

Most importantly, though, the skewer setup is an ideal way to get the crusty outside/tender inside dichotomy that is a primary goal of grilling. To achieve that duality, you should cut whatever you're cooking into big chunks, about an inch or so. That provides about the right shape to just cook through by the time the exterior is properly seared.

There's always the question of whether you should make the skewers out of only one ingredient or you should combine several ingredients on each skewer. We don't have any hard and fast rules for this. Sometimes, as here, we think it works best to have just the meat on the skewer, so it can cook perfectly. Other times we like to combine meat with vegetables, because we are fans of the interesting flavors that result when they cook pressed up against one another.

Oh, and making kebabs provides the chance to break out those ridiculous metal skewers you picked up at some point along the way and rarely use. Or—should you not happen to have a set of those guys tucked away somewhere—you can just use the bamboo skewers that are available everywhere these days. Common wisdom says that you should soak these, but in our experience this is a waste of time because after a minute or so over the fire, the ends dry out and catch fire, anyway. So just use them straight out of the package and, instead of trying to use the (now nonexistent) ends to turn the skewers, just grab hold of the meat with your tongs, pick up the skewer, and turn it over.

# Super-Basic GRILLED LAMB KEBABS

54

## with **Greek Flavors**

55

## with **Turkish Flavors**

57

## with **Italian Flavors**

58

# Spicy Curry-Rubbed Grilled Lamb Kebabs with **Grilled Peaches**

59

# Super-Basic
# GRILLED LAMB KEBABS

**2 pounds boneless lamb leg**

**¹/₄ cup olive oil**

**Kosher salt and freshly cracked black pepper to taste**

 Build a two-level fire in your grill, which means you put all the coals on one side of the grill and leave the other side free of coals. When the flames have died down and the coals are medium-hot (you can hold your hand 6 inches above the grill for 3 to 4 seconds), you're ready to cook.

 Trim the lamb of most but not all the fat and cut into 32 more or less equal chunks. Combine in a bowl with the olive oil, salt, and pepper and toss well to coat.

Thread the lamb chunks onto skewers (8 or so per skewer; they should snuggle up to each other but not be tightly pressed) and place directly over the coals. Cook, turning to expose all 4 sides to the direct heat of the coals, until done to your liking, about 2 minutes per side (8 minutes total) for medium rare. To check for doneness, cut into one of the chunks and check to see if it is done to your liking—remove from the heat when it is a little less done than you want it to be when you eat it, since it will continue to cook after you take if off the grill.

| Serves 4 |

# GRILLED LAMB KEBABS with GREEK FLAVORS

*KEEPING IT SIMPLE HERE; no need for more ingredients, since these have plenty of flavor.*

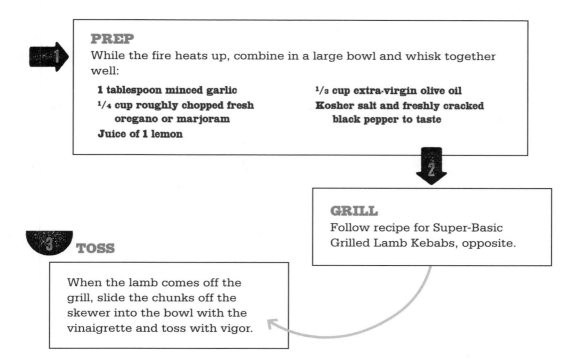

**PREP**

While the fire heats up, combine in a large bowl and whisk together well:

**1 tablespoon minced garlic**
**1/4 cup roughly chopped fresh oregano or marjoram**
**Juice of 1 lemon**

**1/3 cup extra-virgin olive oil**
**Kosher salt and freshly cracked black pepper to taste**

**GRILL**

Follow recipe for Super-Basic Grilled Lamb Kebabs, opposite.

**TOSS**

When the lamb comes off the grill, slide the chunks off the skewer into the bowl with the vinaigrette and toss with vigor.

# GRILLED LAMB KEBABS with TURKISH FLAVORS

GRILL UP some pita for this and serve with a little yogurt on the side. And get yourself some Maras pepper—you'll find lots of other ways to use it. Check out page 234 to learn more about this very cool ingredient.

**1** **PREP**

While the fire heats up, set out in small individual containers:

- ¹/₂ cup dried apricots, diced medium
- 2 tablespoons Maras pepper, or, if you really must, 2 teaspoons other dried chili powder mixed with 1 tablespoon paprika
- 1 teaspoon minced garlic

- 2 tablespoons roughly chopped fresh mint
- ¹/₄ cup extra-virgin olive oil
- Kosher salt and freshly cracked black pepper to taste

**2** **GRILL**

Follow the recipe for Super-Basic Grilled Lamb Kebabs on page 54.

**3** **TOSS**

When the lamb is done, slide the chunks off the skewers into a large bowl, then add each of the other ingredients separately and toss vigorously. Serve warm.

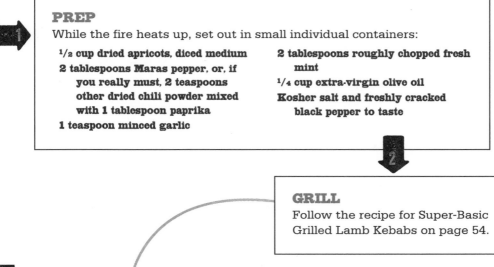

# GRILLED LAMB KEBABS with ITALIAN FLAVORS

*THE PEPPERY BITE of arugula is a nice complement to the lamb. Here it's slightly wilted by the heat of the kebabs, so it ends up being kind of half salad green, half herb.*

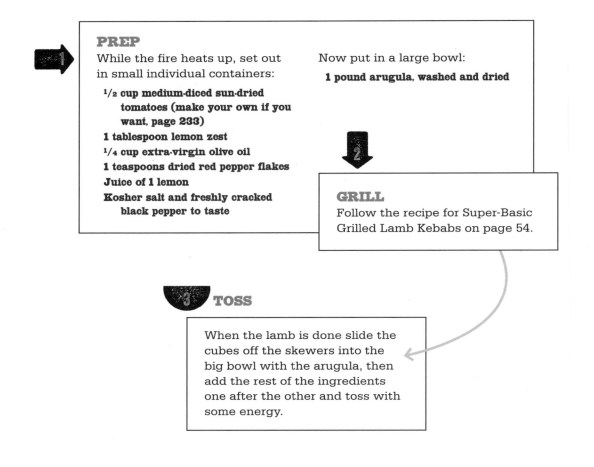

**PREP**

While the fire heats up, set out in small individual containers:

**¹/₂ cup medium-diced sun-dried tomatoes (make your own if you want, page 233)**
**1 tablespoon lemon zest**
**¹/₄ cup extra-virgin olive oil**
**1 teaspoons dried red pepper flakes**
**Juice of 1 lemon**
**Kosher salt and freshly cracked black pepper to taste**

Now put in a large bowl:

**1 pound arugula, washed and dried**

**GRILL**

Follow the recipe for Super-Basic Grilled Lamb Kebabs on page 54.

**TOSS**

When the lamb is done slide the cubes off the skewers into the big bowl with the arugula, then add the rest of the ingredients one after the other and toss with some energy.

# SPICY CURRY-RUBBED GRILLED LAMB KEBABS with GRILLED PEACHES

*OKAY, so peaches aren't really Indian, but they go well with Indian flavors, and they're a good substitute for mangoes. If you're lucky enough to get your hands on some really flavorful mangoes, use them instead.*

### PREP
Chop, measure, and put into small individual containers:

**1 tablespoon roughly chopped garlic**
**¼ cup roughly chopped fresh basil**
**¼ cup red wine vinegar**
**¼ cup extra-virgin olive oil**

**4 to 8 shots of Tabasco, depending on your desire for heat**
**Kosher salt and freshly cracked black pepper to taste**

### GRILL
Follow recipe for Super-Basic Grilled Lamb Kebabs (see page 54), adding to the oil-salt-pepper mixture that goes on the lamb:

**2 tablespoons curry powder (we like Madras)**

Then, when you put the lamb on the grill, also put on, right over the coals:

**2 peaches, pitted and halved**

Cook until the peaches are just slightly charred and softened, 3 to 4 minutes, then remove from the grill, cut each peach half into eighths, and put into a big bowl.

### TOSS

When the lamb skewers are done, slide the lamb chunks off the skewers into the bowl with the peaches, then add the prepped ingredients one by one and toss everything together madly. Taste and add kosher salt and freshly cracked black pepper to taste.

Just before serving, drizzle with:

**1 cup yogurt**
**½ cup minced fresh mint**

PORK

# pork CHOPS

**WE ARE BIG FANS** of all types of pork chops. They have good pork flavor, they're easy to deal with (no butchering or portioning required), they cook pretty quickly, plus they tend to soak up smoky flavor from the grill. That said, there are many options in the world of pork chops, and we had to make some choices here. In the past, we've concentrated on superthin chops (which we call *chuletas*, since that's what they're called in Costa Rica, where we first had them quick-grilled over a wood fire) and the superthick chops, which are almost like mini pork roasts. Each has its distinct advantages. But here we've decided to go for the more standard inch-thick chops, since they are available everywhere and we want these recipes to be superaccessible. And, as always, our choice is to go with bone-in, since the bone not only adds flavor to the chops but also makes them cook a bit more slowly, which is a good thing—not to mention that you get to gnaw on the bone at the end.

Given those parameters, you will have four different types of chops to choose from, depending on which part of the pig's loin they come from. Any will work in these recipes, but the blade and sirloin chops, which come from either end of the loin, tend to be a little tough for grilling. So we recommend you go with rib or center-cut chops, the latter of which are often just called "loin chops." The difference between these two is that the rib has one large eye of loin muscle, while the center-cut chops have some loin muscle and some of the supertender tenderloin muscle. If you want to sound cool you can call your loin chops "pork porterhouse" or "pork T-bones," depending on how big the tenderloin section is, and call your rib chops "pork rib-eyes." Either of these is great. More important than the specific type, though, is that you get a good, hard sear on them, since caramelization will increase and deepen their flavor. This is why we like to cook them right over the coals; if there are flare-ups—and there should be a few—just move the offending chop to the side until the flare-up has died down. Finally, remember that today's pork is safe cooked any way you like it. We prefer it slightly pink, which falls into the medium range. But if you like yours well done, by all means cook it that way—and even if you don't, it's probably a good idea to cook a few that way if you have guests. Old habits die hard, and old culinary habits perhaps hardest of all, which means that people who grew up thinking that pink pork was anathema still tend to shy away from it.

# Super-Basic
# GRILLED PORK CHOPS

64

with **Hoisin-Peanut Sauce**

65

with **Green Apple–Jicama Salsa**

66

with **Corn-Sage Vinaigrette**

68

with **Dried Pineapple–Mint Chutney**

69

**Black Pepper–Crusted Grilled Pork Chops
with Maple-Mustard Glaze and Baby Kale Slaw**

71

# Super-Basic
# GRILLED PORK CHOPS

4 (1-inch-thick) bone-in rib or center-cut loin pork chops, each about 10 to 12 ounces

3 tablespoons olive oil

Kosher salt and freshly cracked black pepper to taste

**1** Build a two-level fire in your grill, which means you put all the coals on one side of the grill and leave the other side free of coals. When the flames have died down, all the coals are covered with gray ash, and the temperature is medium-hot (you can hold your hand 6 inches above the grill for 3 to 4 seconds), you're ready to cook.

**2** Rub the pork chops all over with the oil and sprinkle them generously with the salt and pepper. Put the pork chops on the grill directly over the coals, and cook, turning just once, until done to your liking, about 6 to 8 minutes per side for medium. To check for doneness, cut into the thickest part of one of the chops and peek to see if the meat is done just slightly less than you want it to be when you eat it, since it will continue to cook somewhat more after it comes off the fire.

**3** Take the pork chops off the grill, cover them loosely with foil, and let them rest for 5 minutes, then serve warm.

| Serves 4 |

# GRILLED PORK CHOPS with HOISIN-PEANUT SAUCE

*THIS HAS ASIAN FLAVORS, but it reminds us of the Southern tradition of pork and peanuts, too. Sweet, spicy, a good match with stir-fried bitter greens.*

**1** → **PREP**

While the fire heats up, combine in a large bowl and toss:

- ½ cup hoisin sauce
- ⅓ cup roughly chopped roasted peanuts
- 1 tablespoon minced ginger
- ⅓ cup rice wine vinegar or white wine vinegar
- ⅓ cup soy sauce
- 1 tablespoon brown sugar
- 1 to 2 tablespoons Sriracha or Tabasco, depending on your taste for heat
- ¼ cup roughly chopped fresh cilantro

**2** **GRILL**

Follow the recipe for Super-Basic Grilled Pork Chops, opposite.

**3** **TOP**

When the pork chops have finished their postgrill rest, put them on a platter and spoon just a thin covering of the sauce over each chop, then pass the rest of the sauce in a separate bowl for dipping.

# GRILLED PORK CHOPS with
# GREEN APPLE–JICAMA SALSA

GREEN APPLES are kind of an unusual salsa ingredient, but we think they fit well into the Mexican flavor profile, and they match the jicama crunch for crunch.

## PREP

While the fire heats up, combine in a large bowl and toss well:

- 1 green apple, cored and diced small
- 1 cup small-diced jicama
- 1/4 cup fresh lime juice (from 2 or 3 limes)
- 1/4 cup roughly chopped fresh cilantro

- 1 tablespoon chili powder
- 1 teaspoon ground cumin
- 5 shots Tabasco, or more if you like your food really hot
- Kosher salt and freshly cracked black pepper to taste

## GRILL

Follow the recipe for Super-Basic Grilled Pork Chops on page 64.

## TOP

Spoon a few tablespoons of the salsa onto each individual plate, or spoon about half of it onto a platter. When the pork chops are rested, put them on top of the salsa, then pass the rest of the salsa separately.

# GRILLED PORK CHOPS with CORN-SAGE VINAIGRETTE

*THIS VINAIGRETTE is reminiscent of the piccalilli of the American South, but in vinaigrette form. (By the way, you'll need to have two ears of corn for this, even though you won't use all the kernels from both.)*

## PREP

While the fire heats up, combine in a large bowl and whisk together well:

1 cup kernels (from 2 ears of corn), cut from the cob and blanched in boiling water for 30 seconds

1/3 cup cider vinegar

1/4 cup extra-virgin olive oil

2 tablespoons roughly chopped fresh sage

1 tablespoon sugar

1 tablespoon celery seed

1 teaspoon mustard seed

## GRILL

Follow the recipe for Super-Basic Grilled Pork Chops on page 64.

 TOP

When the pork chops are ready, put them on a platter or individual plates, give the vinaigrette a stir to make sure it hasn't separated, then drizzle it heavily over the chops.

Curve Ball #1

# GRILLED PORK CHOPS with DRIED PINEAPPLE-MINT CHUTNEY

*YOU NEED LOOK no further than the interior of Hawaii—which is actually quite a ways away for most of us—to find the time-honored matchup of pineapple and pork.*

## PREP

While the fire heats up, add to a sauté pan over medium heat:

**2 tablespoons olive oil**

When the oil is hot, add and sauté, stirring occasionally, until transparent, 5 to 6 minutes:

**¼ cup diced onion**

Now add and cook, stirring frequently, for 1 minute:

**1 tablespoon curry powder**
**1 tablespoon minced fresh ginger**

Finally, add:

**½ cup fresh orange juice (from 1 orange)**
**⅓ cup cider vinegar**
**1 tablespoon brown sugar**
**¾ cup medium-diced dried pineapple, dried apricots, or dried mangoes**
**Pinch of cloves**

Bring to a simmer, stirring once in a while, and cook until the mixture just begins to thicken, which might be as little as 5 or as much as 10 minutes. Remove the sauce from the heat and allow it to cool before adding:

**½ cup finely chopped fresh mint**

## GRILL

Follow the recipe for Super-Basic Grilled Pork Chops on page 64.

## TOP

When the pork chops are ready to serve, put them on a platter and top each one with some of the chutney. If you've got chutney left over, pass it separately.

# BLACK PEPPER-CRUSTED GRILLED PORK CHOPS with MAPLE-MUSTARD GLAZE and BABY KALE SLAW

*WHEN YOU THINK of things that go with pork, maple syrup may not be one of them. But we love maple syrup with patty-style breakfast sausage, so we figured it would be a natural. Combine it with mustard, get a little refined Southern with the greens, and you've got a really good dish for company.*

### PREP
Combine in a small bowl and stir together until smooth:

**⅓ cup coarse-ground mustard**
**⅓ cup maple syrup**

Next, put all of these ingredients into a big bowl, toss until well combined, and then lay out on a platter:

**2 cups julienned baby kale or other hearty baby cooking green, such as collards, Swiss chard, or (if you like heat) mustard greens**
**⅓ cup cider vinegar**

**¼ cup extra-virgin olive oil**
**1 tablespoon sugar**
**1 teaspoon minced garlic**
**Kosher salt and freshly cracked black pepper to taste**

### GRILL
Follow the recipe for Super-Basic Grilled Pork Chops (see page 64), but in addition to the salt, rub the chops before they go on the grill with:

**¼ cup freshly cracked black pepper**

### 3 TOP
Sixty seconds before you think the pork chops will be ready to come off of the grill, brush them lightly with the glaze. Then, when the pork chops have been removed from the grill and rested, put them on top of the slaw on the platter. Serve them with the extra glaze as a dipping sauce.

# pork

# SKEWERS

**PORK SKEWERS** have all the same virtues as lamb kebabs (page 54): they cook quickly, are totally adaptable, and are a great way to achieve the crusty outside/ tender inside dichotomy that's the hallmark of great grilled food. As with lamb, here we put only the pork on our skewers, so we can be sure that we cook it just right. (One totally idiosyncratic difference: for some reason, it makes sense to us to refer to them as "kebabs" when made of lamb and "skewers" when pork is involved. Maybe it's that Middle Eastern lamb connection.)

We use either the loin or the tenderloin of pork for skewers, since both are tender enough that the meat doesn't need to spend much time over the fire, which means the tendency to overcook it is much less. Also, either is totally easy to find in any supermarket. (Oddly, the pork tenderloin is much more popular than the tenderloin of any other kind of meat—maybe because it's relatively cheap and still has the twin advantages of being very tender and being a nice size for a quick and easy dinner.) The tenderloin will cook through a tad more quickly than the loin, but it's really very close. In either case, you should buy either a whole tenderloin or a whole center-cut pork loin roast and cut them up into cubes yourself. For more robust pork flavor and a little more chew, you can also use pork butt, which is Chris's choice. As for how much you should cook these skewers, our preference is to leave just a bit of pink in the center; it's no longer unsafe to do so, and if you cook them further than that, they are going to be dry. But, as always, the choice is yours. Just remember that the cubes are going to continue cooking a bit after you take them off the grill, so pull them when they are a bit less done than you want them to be when you eat them.

# Super-Basic
# GRILLED PORK SKEWERS

# Super-Basic
# GRILLED PORK SKEWERS

**2 pounds pork loin or tenderloin, cut into 1-inch chunks**
**¹/₄ cup olive oil**
**Kosher salt and freshly cracked black pepper to taste**

 Build a two-level fire in your grill, which means you put all the coals on one side of the grill and leave the other side free of coals. When the flames have died down, all the coals are covered with gray ash, and the temperature is medium-hot (you can hold your hand 6 inches above the grill for 3 to 4 seconds), you're ready to cook.

 Combine everything in a medium bowl and toss well so the pork gets lightly coated with the oil.

 Thread the pork onto skewers so that they touch but are not jammed too tightly together (8 or so per skewer) and place directly over the coals. Cook, turning occasionally so all sides get nicely seared, until the pork is just done to your liking, 10 to 12 minutes total for the way we like it, which is slightly pink. To check for doneness, cut into one of the pork chunks to be sure it is slightly less done than you like it, since the meat will continue to cook after it's taken off the heat. Slide the pork off the skewers and serve.

| Serves 4 to 6 |

# CORIANDER-CRUSTED GRILLED PORK SKEWERS with MAPLE-MUSTARD BARBECUE SAUCE

*CORIANDER is the working stiff of the spice world—easy to deal with, totally versatile, but with a complex and exotic musky-floral-earthy flavor. This is a good one to get to know.*

### PREP
While the fire heats up, whisk together in a large bowl:

- 1/4 cup maple syrup
- 1/4 cup coarse-ground mustard
- 1/4 cup fresh orange juice (from 1 orange)
- 2 tablespoons roughly chopped fresh oregano

### GRILL
Now follow the recipe for Super-Basic Grilled Pork Skewers (see page 75), rubbing the meat evenly just before they go on the grill with:

- 1/4 cup crushed coriander

 **TOSS**

When the skewers come off the grill, slide the pork chunks into the large bowl, toss everything together until the pork cubes are well coated, and serve.

# GRILLED PORK SKEWERS with
# MANGOES, CHIPOTLE, and LIME

*THIS DISH is a good illustration of the tropical principle of layering fresh flavors; they come at you in waves in every bite.*

### PREP

While the fire heats up, combine in a saucepan, bring to a simmer, simmer gently for 10 minutes, then remove from heat and set aside:

**1 mango, diced medium**
**1/2 cup fresh orange juice (from 1 orange)**
**3 tablespoons minced chipotles in adobo**

Next, chop, measure, and keep separate:

**1/3 cup chopped fresh cilantro**
**1 tablespoon ground cumin**
**1 tablespoon minced garlic**
**1/3 cup fresh lime juice (from 2 limes)**
**Kosher salt and freshly cracked black pepper to taste**

### GRILL

Now follow the rest of the recipe for Super-Basic Grilled Pork Skewers on page 75.

 ### TOSS

When the skewers come off the grill, slide them into the large bowl with the mango-chipotle mixture, add all the other ingredients sequentially, toss like your life depends upon it, and serve.

# GRILLED PORK SKEWERS with GRILLED PEACHES and ARUGULA

*PEACHES were the first fruit we ever grilled, and they're still our favorite. In the late summer when there are lots of them around, do this with them.*

**PREP**

While the fire heats up, whisk together and set aside:

**¹⁄₃ cup extra-virgin olive oil**
**¹⁄₃ cup balsamic vinegar**
**2 tablespoons honey**

Put into a large bowl:

**2 cups arugula**

**GRILL**

Now continue with the recipe for Super-Basic Grilled Pork Skewers on page 75. When you put the skewers on the grill, also put on the grill, cut side down, right along the edge of the fire:

**2 peaches, pitted, halved, and lightly rubbed with vegetable oil**

Grill the peaches until just lightly charred, about 6 minutes, then cut them into medium dice and put into the large bowl with the arugula.

**TOSS**

When the pork skewers come off the grill, slide the pork chunks into the bowl with the peaches, add the dressing, and toss with some vigor so everything is well mixed, and serve.

# HAWAIIAN-STYLE GRILLED PORK SKEWERS

*MAYBE IT'S THE SWEET-AND-SOUR pork dishes we had at all those bad Chinese restaurants in our youth, but we love this combination of flavors.*

## PREP

While the fire heats up, combine in a small saucepan, bring to a simmer, simmer gently for just 1 minute, then remove from the heat and pour into a large bowl:

- **1/3 cup soy sauce**
- **1/3 cup mirin**
- **1 tablespoon minced fresh ginger**

## GRILL

When the fire is ready, but before you grill the pork, place on the fire right over the coals:

- **3 (1-inch-thick) slices fresh pineapple, peeled and cored**

Grill the pineapple until golden, 4 to 5 minutes per side. When the pineapple comes off the grill, cut it into medium dice and put it in the bowl along with the soy sauce mixture.

Now follow the rest of the recipe for Super-Basic Grilled Pork Skewers on page 75.

 TOSS

When the skewers come off the grill, slide them into the large bowl, toss gently to mix, then sprinkle with:

- **1/3 cup thinly sliced scallions, white and light green parts**
- **1/3 cup toasted and chopped macadamia nuts**

# GRILLED PORK and BEANS with SMOKY FENNEL and CHERRY TOMATOES

*NOT THE PORK AND BEANS of your youth, this one has a little chef-y attitude.*

### PREP

While the fire heats up, place in a large bowl, whisk together well, and set aside:

- **¹/₃ cup extra-virgin olive oil**
- **1 tablespoon minced garlic**
- **¹/₃ cup red wine vinegar**
- **2 tablespoons coarse-ground mustard**
- **Kosher salt and freshly cracked black pepper to taste**

Prepare and set side:

- **1 cup grape tomatoes, halved**
- **¹/₂ cup whole parsley leaves**

Now heat in a microwave or in a small pan over low heat until just warm (a little hotter than room temperature):

- **2 cups home-cooked or canned white beans, drained if canned**
- **A sprinkle of kosher salt and freshly cracked black pepper**

Put the beans on a platter or divide among individual plates.

### GRILL

When the fire is ready but before you put the pork onto the grill, put on the fire right over the coals:

- **1 fennel bulb, cut diagonally into slices about 1 inch thick**

Grill the fennel until nicely charred, about 5 minutes per side, then dice medium and put into a large bowl.

Now continue with the recipe for Super-Basic Pork Skewers on page 75.

 ### TOSS and TOP

When the skewers come off the grill, slide the pork into the bowl with the fennel, add the grape tomatoes and parsley, then pour the red wine vinaigrette in and toss, toss, toss. Spoon this mixture over the beans and serve.

# baby back RIBS

**IN EARLIER DAYS**, we were partial to spareribs, but over the years we've also become enamored of baby backs. Nestled under the loin muscle higher up on the hog's rib cage than spareribs, they are not only smaller, but the meat is also leaner and considerably more tender. (Some baby backs have as much as a half inch of supertender loin meat at their tip.) This means that, instead of needing to be cooked for hours over indirect heat like barbecued ribs, these little guys can be cooked directly over the coals in about twenty minutes or so. Obviously, this makes them more convenient for a quick dinner. It also means that they're one of the best things to throw on the grill just before guests arrive, so you can have something to hand them to nibble on along with their first round of beverages. Like their larger cousins the spareribs, baby backs have meat with that unmistakable rich, bacon-y pork flavor, along with a nice bone to gnaw on. Most often these ribs are paired with some sort of thick, sweet-sour barbecue sauce to make the justly famed "sticky ribs." There's nothing wrong with that approach, and we've included a couple of examples here. But pork, to our minds, goes with almost any flavor profile, so we also encourage you to check out some of the other, possibly less traditional, flavor combinations below.

# Super-Basic
# GRILLED BABY BACK RIBS
## 85

## with **Molasses, Jalapeño,** and **Lime**
### 86

## Thai-Style Grilled Baby Back Ribs
### 87

## with **Apricot-Mustard Sauce**
### 88

## with **Maple-Bourbon Barbecue Sauce**
### 89

## Grilled Orange-Glazed Baby Back Ribs
## with **Chile-Peanut Dust**
### 90

# Super-Basic
# GRILLED BABY BACK RIBS

**2 racks baby back ribs, about 3 pounds each**
**Kosher salt and freshly cracked black pepper to taste**

 Build a two-level fire in your grill, which means you put all the coals on one side of the grill and leave the other side free of coals. When the coals are medium (you can hold your hand 6 inches above the grill for 4 to 5 seconds), you're ready to cook.

 Sprinkle the ribs generously with the salt and pepper, place them on the grill directly over the coals, and cook until a peek inside shows that the meat no longer has any pink at the center, about 8 to 10 minutes per side (just to be clear, that's 16 to 20 minutes total).

 Separate into individual ribs and serve.

**Serves 6 as an appetizer, 3 or 4 as an entrée**

# GRILLED BABY BACK RIBS with MOLASSES, JALAPEÑO, and LIME

*EVERYBODY LIKES sweet and sticky—break out lots of napkins for this one.*

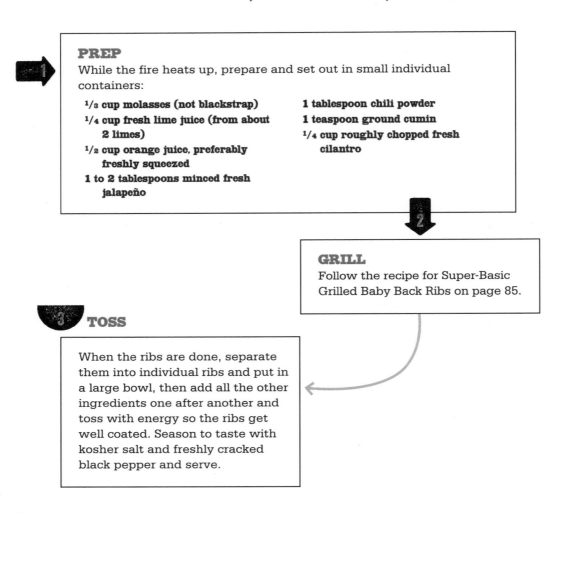

**1**

### PREP

While the fire heats up, prepare and set out in small individual containers:

- 1/3 cup molasses (not blackstrap)
- 1/4 cup fresh lime juice (from about 2 limes)
- 1/2 cup orange juice, preferably freshly squeezed
- 1 to 2 tablespoons minced fresh jalapeño

- 1 tablespoon chili powder
- 1 teaspoon ground cumin
- 1/4 cup roughly chopped fresh cilantro

**2**

### GRILL

Follow the recipe for Super-Basic Grilled Baby Back Ribs on page 85.

**3** TOSS

When the ribs are done, separate them into individual ribs and put in a large bowl, then add all the other ingredients one after another and toss with energy so the ribs get well coated. Season to taste with kosher salt and freshly cracked black pepper and serve.

# THAI-STYLE GRILLED BABY BACK RIBS

*THIS DISH is highly aromatic and a bit spicy, and the lemongrass adds a nice, subtle sourness—but you can leave it out if you can't find it.*

**PREP**

Set out in small individual containers:

- ⅓ cup fish sauce
- ⅓ cup soy sauce
- ⅓ cup fresh lime juice (from about 2 limes)
- 1 tablespoon sugar
- 2 tablespoons minced fresh chile peppers of your choice
- 1 tablespoon minced ginger

- 1 tablespoon minced garlic
- 3 tablespoons finely chopped fresh lemongrass
- 3 tablespoons roughly chopped fresh Thai or Italian basil
- Kosher salt and freshly cracked black pepper to taste

**GRILL**

Follow the recipe for Super-Basic Grilled Baby Back Ribs on page 85.

 **TOSS**

When the ribs come off the grill, cut the racks into individual ribs, put them into a large bowl, then dump in all the other ingredients in random order and toss, toss, toss.

# GRILLED BABY BACK RIBS with APRICOT-MUSTARD SAUCE

SIMPLE, straightforward, but full of flavor. This sauce is a good all-round one—use it on any kind of grilled pork.

## PREP

While the fire heats up, make the glaze: melt in a small saucepan over medium heat (this will take about 5 minutes) or in the microwave:

**⅓ cup apricot preserves**

When the preserves are liquefied, stir in the following and then pour the mixture into a large bowl:

**½ cup coarse-ground mustard**
**⅓ cup cider vinegar**
**2 tablespoons freshly cracked black pepper**
**Kosher salt to taste**

## GRILL

Follow the recipe for Super-Basic Grilled Baby Back Ribs on page 85.

## TOSS

When the rib racks come off the grill, cut them into individual ribs, put them in the large bowl, and toss well. This is another one that you should serve with plenty of paper towels.

# GRILLED BABY BACK RIBS with
# MAPLE-BOURBON BARBECUE SAUCE

*WHAT MAKES THIS a "barbecue sauce"? Ketchup, which is perhaps America's most underrated ingredient.*

### PREP
While the fire heats up, combine in a big bowl and mix together very well:

¹/₂ cup ketchup

¹/₃ cup cider vinegar

¹/₄ cup bourbon of choice

2 tablespoons brown sugar

2 tablespoons maple syrup

1 tablespoon cracked coriander seed

Kosher salt and freshly cracked
   black pepper to taste

### GRILL
Follow the recipe for Super-Basic Grilled Baby Back Ribs on page 85.

 ### TOSS

As you cut the racks into individual ribs, drop the ribs into the big bowl with the sauce and kind of swirl and toss so that the ribs get coated. Now pick each rib up with your tongs and let any extra sauce drip off, then return the ribs to the grill just long enough to slightly caramelize the sauce without burning it, about 30 seconds to 1 minute per side. Serve.

# GRILLED ORANGE-GLAZED BABY BACK RIBS with CHILE-PEANUT DUST

*WHILE YOU'RE AT IT, you might want to make a double or triple batch of the chile-peanut dust, since you have to turn on the oven to make it, and it keeps very well. Try it on anything pork-y.*

## PRE-PREP

To make the Chile-Peanut Dust, preheat oven to 350°F. Combine in a small bowl and mix well:

- **²/₃ cup dry-roasted peanuts, finely chopped**
- **1 tablespoon toasted sesame oil**
- **1¹/₂ teaspoons chili powder**

Put on an unoiled sheet pan and roast, tossing occasionally, until light brown and very fragrant, about 8 to 10 minutes (checking very frequently to prevent burning). Remove and set aside.

## PREP

As the fire heats up, set up in individual containers:

- **¹/₃ cup hoisin sauce**
- **¹/₄ cup soy sauce**
- **¹/₄ cup fresh orange juice (from 1 orange)**
- **2 tablespoons minced ginger**
- **Kosher salt and freshly cracked black pepper to taste**

## GRILL

Follow the recipe for Super-Basic Grilled Baby Back Ribs on page 85.

## TOP

When the rib racks come off the grill, cut them into individual ribs, put in a large bowl, add all of the prep ingredients, and toss vigorously. Lay them out on a platter and top with a mixture of:

- **Chile-Peanut Dust (see above)**
- **¹/₄ cup chopped scallions, white and light green parts**

CHICKEN

# chicken

# BREASTS

**THERE ARE GOOD REASONS** for the popularity of boneless chicken breasts— you can find them in any store, they cook quickly, they're lower in fat and calories than any other part of the chicken, and they are . . . bland and kind of boring. We're sorry, but that's just the plain truth. However, that can also be made into a virtue, since the fact that they have little flavor on their own means that breasts are an excellent foil for all kinds of strong, bold flavor combinations, which is right up our alley. Not to mention that, if you're going to cook chicken breasts, grilling—which by its very nature tends to add flavor to whatever you put over the coals—is probably the very best way to do it. Plus it's a healthy way to cook, so it keeps the faith for those who are eating breasts for that reason. But we do draw the line at skinless chicken breasts; you really need the flavor from the little fat under the skin, plus grilling gives you nice, crisp skin for textural contrast. As a matter of fact, these are starting to sound better and better. A word of caution, though: this is one place to pay close attention to what's happening on the grill, since finding the exact point of doneness is very important here. No one wants undercooked chicken, but it's also easy to overcook the breasts—and if they get dried out, they really aren't worth eating. So start checking doneness early and often, and take them off as soon as they have lost their pinkness, or even when there's just a hint of pinkness at the center, since they will continue to cook after you take them off the grill.

# Super-Basic
# GRILLED CHICKEN BREASTS
## 96

with **Orange-Green Olive Relish**
## 97

with **Cilantro-Lime Vinaigrette**
## 98

with **Maple-Soy Glaze** and **Peanut-Ginger Relish**
## 99

**Curry-Coated Grilled Chicken Breasts** with
**Fresh Mango Chutney**
## 100

# Super-Basic
# GRILLED CHICKEN BREASTS

**8 boneless, skin-on single chicken breasts, about 6 ounces each**
**2 tablespoons olive oil**
**Kosher salt and freshly cracked black pepper to taste**

 Build a two-level fire in your grill, which means you put all the coals on one side of the grill and leave the other side free of coals. When the flames have died down, the charcoal is covered with gray ash, and the fire is medium-hot (you can hold your hand 6 inches above the grill for 3 to 4 seconds), you're ready to cook.

 Rub the chicken breasts with the olive oil and sprinkle generously with the salt and pepper. Grill directly over the coals, turning once, until they are cooked through, about 5 to 7 minutes per side. To check for doneness, make a small cut in the thickest part of the largest breast to be sure it is opaque all the way through.

| Serves 4 to 6 |

# GRILLED CHICKEN BREASTS with ORANGE-GREEN OLIVE RELISH

*CLASSIC Moroccan flavors—a little exotic, a lot easy.*

**1** **PREP**

While the fire heats up, combine in a small bowl and mix together:

- **1 orange, peeled, seeded, and cut into sections**
- **1/2 cup pitted and roughly chopped green olives**
- **1/4 cup extra-virgin olive oil**
- **1/4 cup roughly chopped fresh parsley**
- **1 tablespoon cracked coriander seed**

**2** **GRILL**

Follow the recipe for Super-Basic Grilled Chicken Breasts, opposite.

**3** **TOP**

When the chicken breasts come off the grill, put them on a platter or individual plates and top each with a generous helping of the relish.

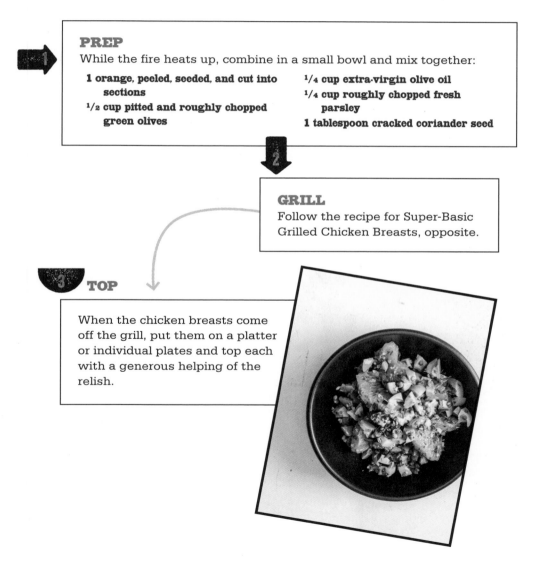

# GRILLED CHICKEN BREASTS with CILANTRO-LIME VINAIGRETTE

*A LITTLE Latin flavor combination creates a close cousin to that takeout Peruvian lime chicken everybody loves.*

### PREP

Just before you think the fire is at the right temperature, whisk the following ingredients together in a medium bowl:

- **¹/₂ cup roughly chopped fresh cilantro**
- **¹/₄ cup extra-virgin olive oil**
- **¹/₄ cup fresh lime juice (from about 2 limes)**

- **1 tablespoon minced garlic**
- **2 tablespoons chili powder**
- **1 tablespoon ground cumin**
- **Kosher salt and freshly cracked black pepper to taste**

### GRILL

Follow the recipe for Super-Basic Grilled Chicken Breasts on page 96.

### TOP

When the chicken breasts come off the grill, put them on a platter or individual plates. Drizzle each one generously with the vinaigrette and pass any remaining vinaigrette separately.

# GRILLED CHICKEN BREASTS with MAPLE-SOY GLAZE and PEANUT-GINGER RELISH

*ALTHOUGH MAPLE isn't part of the Asian larder, it turns out that it goes really well with soy sauce, so we combine them, along with a deconstructed Southeast Asian peanut sauce.*

### PREP

While the fire heats up, make the glaze. Combine in a small bowl and mix well:

- **1/3 cup maple syrup**
- **1/3 cup soy**

Then make the relish. Combine in a small bowl and mix well:

- **1/2 cup toasted and chopped unsalted peanuts**
- **2 tablespoons chopped fresh ginger**
- **1/4 cup roughly chopped fresh cilantro**
- **1 tablespoon (or more if you really like heat) Sriracha or chile sambal**
- **2 tablespoons fresh lime juice (from about 1 lime)**
- **Kosher salt and freshly cracked black pepper to taste**

### GRILL

Follow the recipe for Super-Basic Grilled Chicken Breasts on page 96. When the chicken breasts come off the grill, apply the glaze to both sides, then put them back over the coals and cook just until the glaze is caramelized, about 30 minutes per side.

### TOP

Remove to a platter or individual plates, then spoon a couple of tablespoons of the relish over each breast and serve, passing any remaining relish separately.

*Curve Ball*

# CURRY-COATED GRILLED CHICKEN BREASTS with FRESH MANGO CHUTNEY

YOU MIGHT be able to get a cup of diced mango out of one large fruit, but buy two just to be safe—lord knows there are plenty of other ways to use them.

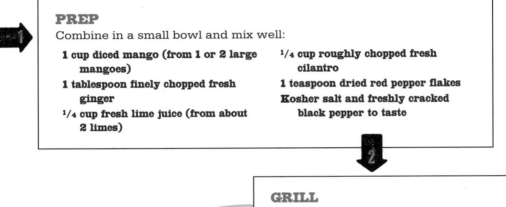

## PREP

Combine in a small bowl and mix well:

**1 cup diced mango (from 1 or 2 large mangoes)**

**1 tablespoon finely chopped fresh ginger**

**¼ cup fresh lime juice (from about 2 limes)**

**¼ cup roughly chopped fresh cilantro**

**1 teaspoon dried red pepper flakes**

**Kosher salt and freshly cracked black pepper to taste**

## GRILL

Follow the recipe for Super-Basic Grilled Chicken Breasts (see page 96), but before the chicken goes on the grill, press onto it evenly:

**2 tablespoons curry powder**

## TOP

When the chicken breasts come off the grill, place them on a platter or individual plates, spoon a bit of chutney over each one, and sprinkle with:

**¼ cup toasted dried coconut**

**¼ cup toasted and chopped macadamia nuts**

**1 tablespoon lime zest**

# chicken THIGHS

**THIS JUST MIGHT BE** our favorite part of the chicken. It has more richly flavorful meat than the breast, but it's a lot less bony and meatier than the other dark meat pieces. As with all other things, we prefer to grill thighs bone-in, because it adds more flavor. Bone-in thighs are much easier to cook than a bone-in chicken breast or leg—with the leg, the joint takes a long time to cook so the temptation is to overdo it, while the breast is an uneven thickness, which always makes for tough cooking, plus it's so lean that it, too, is very prone to overcooking. But the thigh is pretty uniform in shape and it has more fat to prevent it from cooking too fast. What we're getting at here is that the thighs are the most flavorful, convenient, and forgiving part of the chicken. Plus thighs are a good portion size—most people will eat two, but it's easy to serve up a platter and let everyone decide how many they want. But maybe the best thing about them is that they have a really good ratio of skin to meat; the only chicken part with a better ratio is the wing, which doesn't lend itself as well to entrée treatments. One of the best things about having a good proportion of skin is that you also get enough fat to give some real flavor and to keep the meat moist during cooking. The bad part of this, of course, is that the thigh is more prone to flare-ups when it's over the coals. So you have to pay some attention while you're grilling these, and when flare-ups do occur, simply move that piece to the part of the grill with no coals until the flames die down. This is one place where you're going to be glad you have a good pair of tongs for moving things around quickly and easily on the grill.

# Super-Basic
## GRILLED CHICKEN THIGHS

104

with **Mustard-Marjoram Vinaigrette**

105

with **Apricot-Chile Glaze** and **Minted Couscous**

107

with **Bacon-Pecan Relish**

108

with **Chunky Peach-Bourbon Barbecue Sauce**
and **Hot and Sour Lime Slaw**

111

with **Spinach, Yogurt**, and **Grapes**

113

# Super-Basic
# GRILLED CHICKEN THIGHS

8 medium bone-in, skin-on chicken thighs, each about 6 ounces

3 tablespoons olive oil

Kosher salt and freshly cracked black pepper to taste

**1** Build a two-level fire in your grill, which means you put all the coals on one side of the grill and leave the other side free of coals. When the flames have died down, all the coals are covered with gray ash, and the temperature is medium (you can hold your hand 6 inches above the grill for 4 to 5 seconds), you're ready to cook.

**2** Rub the chicken thighs with the olive oil and sprinkle generously with the salt and pepper. Grill directly over the coals, turning once, until they are cooked through, about 8 to 10 minutes per side. (If flare-ups occur, move the thighs to the part of the grill with no coals until the flames die down. If you have lots of flare-ups, move the thighs into a kind of semicircle around the outer edge of the coals and cook them there.) To check for doneness, make a small cut in the thickest part of the thigh to be sure it is opaque all the way through.

**Serves 4 to 6**

# GRILLED CHICKEN THIGHS with MUSTARD-MARJORAM VINAIGRETTE

*MARJORAM is an underused herb—a kind of more aromatic, delicate-flavored oregano. Chris voted it Herb of the Year in 2009, but he's still waiting for it to come into its rightful popularity.*

**PREP**

While the fire heats up, whisk together in a really big bowl until well incorporated:

¹/₄ cup coarse-ground mustard
¹/₃ cup extra-virgin olive oil
¹/₄ cup balsamic vinegar
3 tablespoons roughly chopped fresh marjoram (or oregano)

2 teaspoons freshly cracked black pepper
Kosher salt to taste

**2**

**GRILL**

Follow the recipe for Super-Basic Grilled Chicken Thighs, opposite.

**3 TOSS**

When the thighs come off the grill, place them in the bowl with the vinaigrette and toss them around until the thighs are well covered.

# GRILLED CHICKEN THIGHS with
# APRICOT-CHILE GLAZE and MINTED COUSCOUS

*WE LOVE USING apricot preserves as a base for glazes. Here the spicy chile sambal creates the classic sweet and hot combination.*

### PREP

While the fire heats up, make the glaze. Combine in a small saucepan over medium heat until the preserves are liquefied, about 5 minutes:

- **1/2 cup apricot preserves**
- **1/4 cup chile sambal or Sriracha**
- **1/4 cup cider vinegar**

To make the couscous combine:

- **1 cup boiling water**
- **1 cup instant couscous**

Cover and set aside for 20 minutes, fluff with a fork and stir in:

- **1/2 cup roughly chopped fresh mint**
- **Kosher salt and freshly cracked black pepper to taste**

### GRILL

Follow the recipe for Super-Basic Grilled Chicken Thighs on page 104.

### TOSS and TOP

When the chicken thighs come off the grill, place them in a bowl, add the glaze, and toss. Return them to the grill and cook briefly, just until the glaze is caramelized, about 30 seconds per side. Take them off the grill and serve them over the couscous; if you've got any glaze left, drizzle it over the top.

# GRILLED CHICKEN THIGHS with BACON-PECAN RELISH

BACON may not be your typical relish ingredient, but here it creates a value-added meat-on-meat preparation, with a little Southern twist in the form of pecans. In fact, you might want to make a double batch of this relish while you're at it — it keeps for a few days, and it goes with any form of chicken.

## PREP

1

While the fire heats up, make the relish. Combine in a sauté pan over medium heat and cook until just a bit short of crisp:

**1/2 pound bacon, diced small**

Pour off all but about 1 tablespoon of the fat and add:

**1/4 cup diced red onion**

Return the pan to the heat and cook, stirring once in a while, until the onion is soft, about 5 minutes. Remove from the heat and stir in:

**1/3 cup toasted and roughly chopped pecans**
**1/2 cup roughly chopped fresh parsley**
**1 tablespoon orange zest**
**3 tablespoons extra-virgin olive oil**
**3 tablespoons fresh orange juice (from 1 orange)**
**2 tablespoons cider vinegar**
**Kosher salt and freshly cracked black pepper to taste**

2

## GRILL

Follow the recipe for Super-Basic Grilled Chicken Thighs on page 104.

3 TOP

When the chicken thighs are done, put them on a platter or individual plates and spoon some relish over each one. If you've got relish left, pass it in a small bowl.

# GRILLED CHICKEN THIGHS with CHUNKY PEACH-BOURBON BARBECUE SAUCE and HOT AND SOUR LIME SLAW

*IF YOU'RE MAKING THIS at a time of year when the peaches in the store are not so great, you can actually use frozen peaches. The sour slaw is a nice counterpoint to the rather sweet barbecue sauce, but be aware that it's very intense, really more of a relish—a couple of tablespoons will be enough for most folks. (If you have any left over, it's excellent on hot dogs.)*

### PREP

While the fire heats up, make the barbecue sauce. Cook in a sauté pan over medium heat, stirring occasionally, for 3 to 4 minutes:

**1 tablespoon olive oil**
**1 peach, diced small**

Add and cook for 1 additional minute, stirring a bit more frequently:

**1 tablespoon minced fresh ginger**

Remove from the heat and stir in:

**¼ cup bourbon**
**¼ cup cider vinegar**

Return the sauce to medium heat and cook for an additional 2 minutes, then add:

**2 tablespoons brown sugar**
**½ cup ketchup**
**1 teaspoon freshly cracked black pepper**

Cook the sauce, stirring frequently, for a final 3 minutes, then set aside to cool to room temperature.

(continued )

(Grilled Chicken Thighs with Chunky Peach-Bourbon Barbecue Sauce, continued)

**PREP,
cont'd**

Now make the slaw. Combine in a medium bowl and toss together well:

**2 cups grated green cabbage (about one-quarter of a medium head, cored)**
**¹/₃ cup fresh lime juice (from 2 to 3 limes)**
**1 tablespoon sugar**
**1 to 2 tablespoons minced fresh chile pepper of your choice**
**1 tablespoon cracked coriander seed**
**Kosher salt and freshly cracked black pepper to taste**

**GRILL**
Follow the recipe for Super-Basic Grilled Chicken Thighs on page 104.

 **TOSS and TOP**

When the chicken thighs come off the grill, place them in a big bowl, add the barbecue sauce, and toss to coat. Put them on a big platter and either top each with a tablespoon or two of the slaw or pass it separately for folks to help themselves.

# GRILLED CHICKEN THIGHS with SPINACH, YOGURT, and GRAPES

*THIS DISH is a good illustration of the principle that "spicy" doesn't have to mean "hot." It's also a guaranteed crowd-pleaser, exotic without being weird.*

## PREP

While the fire heats up, prepare the following and set out in small individual containers:

**1 tablespoon minced fresh ginger**
**1 tablespoon minced fresh garlic**
**1 tablespoon cracked coriander seed**
**1 tablespoon mustard seed**
**1 tablespoon ground curry powder**
**1/2 cup halved seedless green grapes**
**1 cup yogurt**
**Kosher salt and freshly cracked black pepper to taste**

Then put into a really big bowl:

**12 ounces baby spinach**

## GRILL

Follow the recipe for Super-Basic Grilled Chicken Thighs on page 104.

 TOSS

As soon as the thighs are done, add them to the big bowl with the spinach (it's good if the thighs slightly wilt some of the spinach), then add each of the other ingredients in sequence, toss like a maniac, and serve.

# chicken WINGS

**WHEN YOU SAY "CHICKEN WINGS,"** most people think "party." And they're not wrong. Wings are pretty much the ideal party food—cheap, tasty, easy to cook, small enough to serve as a bar food-type snack but substantial enough to dull guests' hunger. And maybe best of all, you have to eat them with your hands, which fits the relaxed atmosphere of any party we'd want to go to. (Seriously, have you ever seen anyone eat a wing with a utensil? Some people even eat pizza with a knife and fork. But wings? Never.)

Even if you're not a party person, though, wings should have a prominent place in your grilling repertoire because, in addition to all the virtues we listed above, grilled wings are just plain delicious. To our minds, they may be the best part of the chicken, which is somewhat ironic since people used to either toss them or use them just for stock. They've got the highest ratio of skin to meat, and there's really not anything much tastier than that just slightly greasy, rich flavor of the skin of a properly grilled wing. Plus wings have great texture, since the high heat of the fire quickly renders most of the fat and makes the skin beautifully crisp.

Our friend Ihsan Gurdal, owner of Formaggio Kitchen in Cambridge, Massachusetts, and a dedicated griller, has made chicken wings his specialty over the past few years. In fact, it's not unusual for him to serve wings as the main part of a dinner instead of just a premeal snack. We've found this to be an excellent idea as well, and we're giving you plenty of razzle-dazzles for wings so you can, should you choose, even serve a variety of different flavors. Because yet another virtue of chicken wings is that their mild flavor makes them a perfect vehicle for strong flavorings of any kind.

We like to cut the wings into thirds before we grill them. We then freeze the little tips to use when we make stock, and end up with two meaty little winglets that are easier to eat than if you left the wings whole. Also, the two portions lie flat on the grill, so they get evenly cooked. On the other hand, if you're a person who dislikes prep, you can also grill the wings whole. Your choice.

# Super-Basic GRILLED CHICKEN WINGS

# Super-Basic
# GRILLED CHICKEN WINGS

**3 pounds jumbo chicken wings**
**Kosher salt and freshly cracked black pepper to taste**

 Build a two-level fire in your grill, which means you put all the coals on one side of the grill and leave the other side free of coals. When the flames have died down, the coals are covered with gray ash, and the fire is medium-hot (you can hold your hand 6 inches above the grill for 4 to 5 seconds), you're ready to cook.

 Cut the wings into 3 sections, saving the tips for stock. Sprinkle the 2 larger sections with the salt and pepper and grill directly over the coals, flipping occasionally, until cooked through, about 10 to 12 minutes. To check for doneness, cut into one of the wing sections at the joint; there should be no pinkness. Serve hot.

**Serves 4 to 6 as an appetizer**

# GRILLED CHICKEN WINGS with FRESH HERBS, GARLIC, and LEMON

*As spicy as you want them to be, these are one of summer's best party starters.*

**1 PREP**

While the fire heats up, prepare the following and set out in small individual containers:

- ⅓ cup extra-virgin olive oil
- 1 tablespoon roughly chopped fresh garlic
- ¼ cup freshly chopped herbs, any one or a combination of any of the following: basil, parsley, marjoram, oregano, or thyme

- 8 to 12 shots of Tabasco, depending on your appetite for heat
- Juice of 1 lemon (about ¼ cup)

**2 GRILL**

Follow recipe for Super-Basic Grilled Chicken Wings on page 117.

**3 TOSS**

When the wings come off the grill, dump them into a very large bowl, add all of the prepped ingredients one after the other, and toss as if your party's life depended on it. Serve hot.

# LATIN-STYLE GRILLED CHICKEN WINGS

*IF YOU CAN'T FIND chipotles in adobo, use dried ones hydrated in a little oil; if you can't find those, either, you can use jalapeños and a couple of drops of Liquid Smoke. But you should try to find the real thing.*

### PREP

While the fire heats up, prepare the following ingredients and put them in small individual containers:

- 1/3 cup extra-virgin olive oil
- 1 tablespoon minced fresh garlic
- 2 tablespoons minced chipotle peppers in adobo (or less, if you don't like spicy food that much)
- 1 tablespoon ground cumin
- 1/4 cup roughly chopped fresh cilantro
- 1/4 cup fresh lime juice (from about 2 limes)
- Kosher salt and freshly cracked black pepper to taste

### GRILL

Follow the recipe for Super-Basic Grilled Chicken Wings on page 117.

### TOSS

When the wings come off the grill, put them into a giant bowl. Now add in each of the prepped ingredients one after the other, toss everything with some real energy, and check to see if they need more salt. Add it if they do, then serve.

# HOISIN-GLAZED GRILLED CHICKEN WINGS

*ALWAYS HAVE hoisin sauce in your pantry—it's one of those great condiments that adds a ton of complex flavor all by itself.*

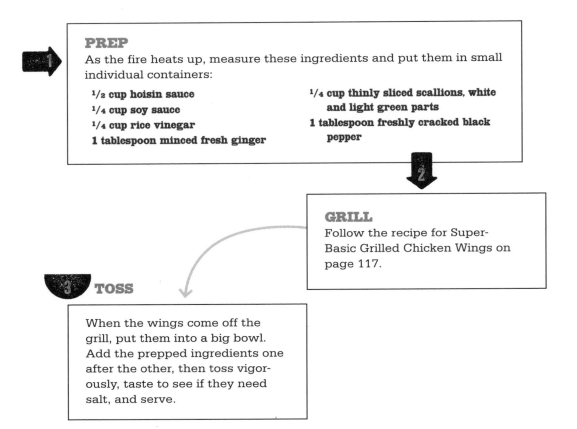

**1** **PREP**
As the fire heats up, measure these ingredients and put them in small individual containers:

1/2 cup hoisin sauce

1/4 cup soy sauce

1/4 cup rice vinegar

1 tablespoon minced fresh ginger

1/4 cup thinly sliced scallions, white and light green parts

1 tablespoon freshly cracked black pepper

**2** **GRILL**
Follow the recipe for Super-Basic Grilled Chicken Wings on page 117.

**3** **TOSS**
When the wings come off the grill, put them into a big bowl. Add the prepped ingredients one after the other, then toss vigorously, taste to see if they need salt, and serve.

# SPICY SOUTHEAST ASIAN-STYLE GRILLED CHICKEN WINGS

*HERE YOU GET lots of flavors coming at you all at once, in that classic Southeast Asian fashion. Don't skip any of the herbs; they really make the dish.*

## PREP

While the fire heats up, measure out each of these ingredients, put them in small individual containers, and line them up next to a large bowl on the counter or next to the grill:

¹/₄ cup fish sauce

¹/₄ cup soy sauce

¹/₄ cup fresh lime juice (from about 2 limes)

2 tablespoons minced fresh ginger

1 tablespoon minced garlic

3 tablespoons Sriracha or chile sambal, or less or more according to your taste for heat

2 tablespoons sugar

¹/₄ cup freshly chopped basil

¹/₄ cup freshly chopped cilantro

¹/₄ cup freshly chopped mint

## GRILL

Follow the recipe for Super-Basic Grilled Chicken Wings on page 117.

## TOSS

Put the grilled wings into that large bowl, then pour or dump each of the other ingredients in, one by one, ending with the herbs. Toss energetically, check for salt, and serve.

# JERK WINGS FROM HELL

*CAREFUL: These wings will burn your head off. We're not kidding. We're working with a kind of Jamaican jerk thing here, but hotter. Much hotter.*

## PREP

While the fire heats up, combine in a food processor or blender and puree until smooth:

- ¼ cup dried thyme
- ¼ cup dried oregano
- ¼ cup dried basil
- ¼ cup extra-virgin olive oil
- ¼ cup fresh orange juice (from 1 orange)
- ¼ cup cheap yellow mustard
- 1 tablespoon minced garlic
- 10 Scotch Bonnet peppers (okay to substitute habanero peppers)

## GRILL

Divide the wings into sections as directed in step 2 of the recipe for Super-Basic Grilled Chicken Wings (see page 117). Rub the Scotch Bonnet paste all over the wing sections, then put the wings on the cooler side of the fire and grill until just cooked through, about 10 to 12 minutes.

CAUTION: These wings are likely to burn because of the heavy rub—move them around a lot and check to be sure they aren't burning; if they are, move well off the fire and let them finish cooking.

## TOP

When the wings are done, remove them from the grill and sprinkle them with:

- ¼ cup chopped scallions (about 2 scallions), white and light green parts only
- 1 tablespoon mustard seeds
- 1 teaspoon allspice

Serve with the antidote (orange creamsicles) on the side.

# chicken SKEWERS

**THIS SET OF RECIPES** is inspired by yakitori, the justly famed grilled chicken skewers of Japan. But unlike Japanese practitioners of the yakitori art, who put every part of the chicken from hearts to gizzards to skin on their skewers, we restrict ourselves to the more pedestrian (and readily available) breast and thigh meat. We prefer to use thigh meat ourselves, since it's more flavorful and less prone to overcooking, but feel free to use breast meat if that's what you prefer; you'll just need to be a bit more watchful to make sure it doesn't overcook, and, of course, cook it a couple of minutes less. Whichever type of chicken you use, these skewers are going to have plenty of flavor, since we have paired the meat with boldly flavored ingredients, from Sriracha to smoked paprika to a ton of garlic. In fact, precisely because of the chicken's relatively mild taste, these skewers offer an excellent opportunity to play around with flavor footprints from various parts of the world. We've gone Italian, Spanish, Thai, and Caribbean, but once you get the hang of it, you can adapt them to whichever particular flavor profile is your favorite.

# Super-Basic
# GRILLED CHICKEN SKEWERS

# Super-Basic
# GRILLED CHICKEN SKEWERS

**2 pounds boneless chicken breasts or thighs, cut into 1-inch chunks**

**3 tablespoons olive oil**

**Kosher salt and freshly cracked black pepper to taste**

 Build a two-level fire in your grill, which means you put all the coals on one side of the grill and leave the other side free of coals. When the flames have died down, all the coals are covered with gray ash, and the temperature is medium (you can hold your hand 6 inches above the grill for 4 to 5 seconds), you're ready to cook.

 Combine the chicken, olive oil, salt, and pepper in a large bowl and toss well to coat, then thread the chicken onto the skewers so they press up against one another but aren't jammed together. Put the skewers on the grill directly over the coals and cook, rolling the skewers around every 3 to 4 minutes to ensure all the sides are more or less evenly exposed to the heat, until lightly seared, a total of 10 to 12 minutes for breast meat, 12 to 14 minutes for thigh meat. To check for doneness, just make a small cut and peek inside to be sure it is opaque all the way through with no trace of pink.

| Serves 4 to 6 |

# GRILLED CHICKEN SKEWERS with ENDIVE and SUN-DRIED TOMATOES

*WITH A LITTLE pleasant bitterness from the endive, this makes a simple light lunch entrée. Or if you want, you can serve it as a dinner appetizer.*

**PREP**

While the fire heats up, combine in a large bowl and mix well:

1 medium-size endive, washed, dried, and thinly sliced

1/2 cup sun-dried tomatoes, diced medium

1/4 cup extra-virgin olive oil

1/4 cup fresh lemon juice (from 1 lemon)

Kosher salt and freshly cracked black pepper to taste

**GRILL**

Follow the recipe for Super-Basic Grilled Chicken Skewers, opposite.

**TOSS**

When the chicken comes off the grill, push the cubes off the skewers into a big bowl (if it's the same one you used to coat the chicken with oil, wash it well first). Add each of the prepped ingredients sequentially but quickly, and then toss enthusiastically to mix evenly.

# GRILLED CHICKEN SKEWERS with DECONSTRUCTED PESTO

*TASTE THIS and see if it doesn't have a more vibrant flavor than regular made-ahead pesto. To us, it clearly makes the case for putting everything together at the last minute.*

**PREP**

While the fire heats up, prepare the following ingredients, keeping them separate in small individual containers:

1 cup grated Parmesan cheese (about 2 ounces)

1/2 cup roughly chopped fresh basil

1/4 cup toasted pine nuts

1 tablespoon minced garlic

1/3 cup extra-virgin olive oil

Kosher salt and freshly cracked black pepper to taste

**GRILL**

Follow the recipe for Super-Basic Grilled Chicken Skewers on page 126.

**TOSS**

When the chicken comes off the grill, put it into a large bowl (washing the bowl first if it's the same one you used to toss the chicken with oil), add each of the prepared ingredients one after another, starting with the cheese, then toss enthusiastically to mix.

# GRILLED CHICKEN SKEWERS with PEACHES, SMOKED PAPRIKA, and SHERRY VINEGAR

*SHERRY VINEGAR is one of those ingredients that adds deep flavor anywhere it's used. We particularly like it with its fellow Spaniard, smoked paprika. In this dish, Chris continues his love affair with peaches—but Doc recommends mangoes.*

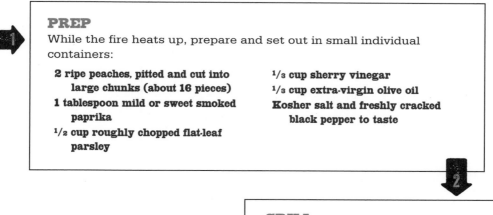

**PREP**

While the fire heats up, prepare and set out in small individual containers:

2 ripe peaches, pitted and cut into large chunks (about 16 pieces)

1 tablespoon mild or sweet smoked paprika

1/2 cup roughly chopped flat-leaf parsley

1/3 cup sherry vinegar

1/3 cup extra-virgin olive oil

Kosher salt and freshly cracked black pepper to taste

**GRILL**

Follow the recipe for Super-Basic Grilled Chicken Skewers on page 126.

 **TOSS**

When the chicken comes off the grill, push the cubes off the skewers into a giant bowl, add all the prepped ingredients one after the other, and toss forcefully.

*Curve Ball*

# GRILLED SESAME CHICKEN SKEWERS with ASPARAGUS, GINGER, and SRIRACHA

*LOTS OF VIBRANT Asian flavors going on here, playing against the mellow asparagus. Use your rasp grater for the orange peel.*

## 1 PREP

While the fire heats up, in a large stockpot filled with boiling water over medium-high heat, blanch until just tender, 2 to 3 minutes:

**20 asparagus spears, ends trimmed**

Remove the asparagus from the water and quickly place it in a bowl filled with ice-cold water to stop the cooking. Cut each spear into 4 pieces and set aside.

Next, prepare and set out in small individual containers:

**2 tablespoons minced fresh ginger**
**1 teaspoon minced garlic**
**¼ cup Sriracha**
**⅓ cup soy sauce**
**1 teaspoon sugar**

## 2 GRILL

Follow the recipe for Super-Basic Grilled Chicken Skewers (see page 126) but replace the olive oil, kosher salt, and freshly cracked black pepper with:

**1 tablespoon toasted sesame oil**
**2 tablespoons vegetable oil**
**1 tablespoon freshly cracked white pepper**
**Kosher salt to taste**

## 3 TOSS

When the chicken comes off the grill, push the cubes off the skewers into a giant bowl, add all the prepped ingredients sequentially, toss with some enthusiasm, and finally sprinkle with:

**¼ cup toasted sesame seeds**
**2 tablespoons orange zest**

# whole CHICKENS

**COOKING WHOLE BIRDS** is bit of a departure for this book, since you cook them by smoke-roasting rather than grilling. But we really like smoky whole chickens, so we figured we'd bend the rules a bit. After all, this is one of those impressive culinary moments when you lift the dome off the grill and the gorgeous, golden mahogany chicken comes out, and you slice into a leg and the juices come dripping out and the smell is so good, and . . . well, you get the idea. In fact, we like them so much that the recipes here call for two chickens. This is enough for six people, so if you have only two or three (or even four), you will probably not eat all of both of them; this means that you have enough for another meal or two, which is always a good thing. What we do here is coat each chicken with a rub, which enhances the skin by giving it a concentrated, flavorful crust. Then for even bolder flavors, we provide a dipping sauce for each version. Of course, you can skip one or the other if you want to save a bit of time—though you can easily make the rubs hours, days, or weeks in advance, then keep them on hand for when the mood strikes. A word about the method here: since this is a variation on roasting, the temperature inside the grill is more important than with regulation grilling, so we specify the amount of charcoal to use for the initial fire and when reloading. We thought it most useful to use a common object to give you an idea of how much to use, so we chose a shoe box. As it turns out, a large chimney starter also holds about the same as a relatively large shoe box, so if you have one of those you're all set. And if your grill has a thermometer on it, the temperature should stay at somewhere in the 325° to 375°F range for most of the time.

# Super-Basic
## SMOKE-ROASTED WHOLE CHICKENS

# Super-Basic
# SMOKE-ROASTED WHOLE CHICKENS

2 whole chickens, about 3 pounds each
3 tablespoons olive oil
Kosher salt and freshly cracked black pepper to taste
2 lemons, halved

 Build a fire well over to one side of your grill, using enough charcoal to fill 1¼ shoe boxes (one whole large chimney starter full). When the flames have died down, all the coals are covered with gray ash, and the temperature is medium (you can hold your hand 6 inches above the coals for 4 to 5 seconds), you're ready to cook.

Place the chickens on your work surface, breast side up, and rub all over with the olive oil, then the salt and pepper, pressing gently to be sure the seasoning adheres to the chicken. Place the chickens, breast side down, on the side of the grill away from the coals, being careful that none of the meat is directly over the coals. Put the lid on the grill with the vents open one-quarter of the way. Cook

| Serves 6 |

for 30 minutes, then turn the chickens breast side up, add another half shoe box (just under half of a large chimney starter) full of fresh charcoal, and continue cooking for 30 to 45 minutes. To check for doneness, cut into the thickest part of the thigh, all the way to the bone, and look inside to be sure it is opaque all the way through with no trace of pink.

 Take the chickens off the grill, cover them loosely with foil, and let them rest for about 15 minutes. When the chickens have had their rest, carve each into 6 pieces, squeeze the lemon halves over them, and serve.

# SMOKE-ROASTED WHOLE CHICKENS with SOUTH CAROLINA–STYLE BARBECUE SAUCE

IN THE SOUTH, there are many types of barbecue sauce. This one, which has a fair amount of mustard in it, is typical of parts of South Carolina where there were a large number of German immigrants, who liked mustard, it seems, with just about everything.

## PREP

While the fire heats up, combine in a large bowl and mix well:

- 1/2 cup ketchup
- 1/2 cup coarse-ground mustard
- 1/4 cup cider vinegar
- 2 tablespoons brown sugar
- 1 tablespoon Worcestershire sauce
- 1 tablespoon Tabasco

To make the rub, combine in a separate bowl and mix together:

- 1/4 cup brown sugar
- 1/4 cup ground coriander
- 2 tablespoons ground cumin
- 2 tablespoons kosher salt
- 2 tablespoons freshly cracked black pepper

## GRILL

Follow the recipe for Super-Basic Smoke-Roasted Whole Chickens (see page 134) but rub the chickens with the brown sugar rub before placing them on the grill.

## 3 TOP

When the chickens are all rested and ready to go, carve each into 6 pieces, drizzle with the barbecue sauce, and serve the rest as a dipping sauce.

# CURRY-RUBBED SMOKE-ROASTED WHOLE CHICKENS
## with FRESH TOMATO-MINT CHUTNEY

*FRESH MINT CHUTNEY goes perfectly with the deep flavors of the smoke-roasted chicken. This makes a really nice chicken salad (with some green grapes) if you have any left over.*

### PREP

While the fire heats up, combine in a large bowl and mix well:

**1 cup diced tomatoes**

**1 cup peeled, seeded, and diced cucumber**

**2 tablespoons fresh ginger**

**1 tablespoon minced fresh chiles of your choice**

**1/3 cup roughly chopped fresh mint**

**1 tablespoon cumin seeds**

**1/2 cup fresh lemon juice (from 2 lemons)**

**Kosher salt and freshly cracked black pepper to taste**

To make the curry rub, combine in a separate bowl and mix together:

**1/3 cup curry powder**

**1/4 cup ground ginger**

**2 tablespoons turmeric**

**2 tablespoons chili powder**

**2 tablespoons kosher salt**

### GRILL

Follow the recipe for Super-Basic Smoke-Roasted Whole Chickens (see page 134) but rub the chickens with the curry rub after the salt and pepper.

### TOP

When the chickens have rested, carve each into 6 pieces and serve topped with (or laid on top of, if you want to be au courant) the chutney.

# LATIN-FLAVORED SMOKE-ROASTED WHOLE CHICKENS
## with LIME-CHIPOTLE BARBECUE SAUCE

*SERVE THIS ONE with warm grilled tortillas and rice and beans. That's your awesome summer Latin meal right there.*

### PREP

While the fire heats up, combine in a large bowl and mix well:

- **³/₄ cup ketchup**
- **¹/₃ cup fresh lime juice (from 3 limes)**
- **3 tablespoons pureed chipotle peppers in adobo**
- **¹/₃ cup roughly chopped fresh cilantro**

To make the Latin rub, combine in a separate bowl and mix together:

- **¹/₄ cup chili powder**
- **¹/₄ cup cumin seeds**
- **¹/₄ cup dried oregano**
- **3 tablespoons minced garlic**
- **¹/₄ cup extra-virgin olive oil**

### GRILL

Follow the recipe for Super-Basic Smoke-Roasted Whole Chickens (see page 134) but rub the chickens with the Latin rub after the salt and pepper.

 TOP

When the chickens are ready to go, carve each into 6 pieces. To serve, drizzle each with a bit of the barbecue sauce and pass the rest in a small bowl for individual dipping.

# SMOKE-ROASTED WHOLE CHICKENS with MANY ASIAN FLAVORS

*IF YOU THINK you're not going to eat all of both chickens, make some rice and put it aside—that way, you can have smoky Asian fried rice the next night.*

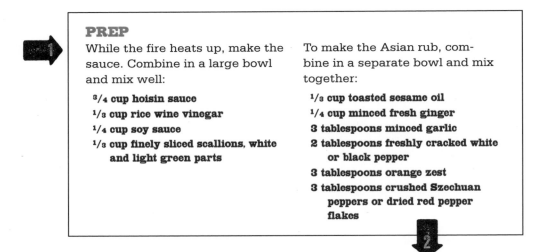

## PREP

While the fire heats up, make the sauce. Combine in a large bowl and mix well:

- ³/₄ **cup hoisin sauce**
- ¹/₃ **cup rice wine vinegar**
- ¹/₄ **cup soy sauce**
- ¹/₃ **cup finely sliced scallions, white and light green parts**

To make the Asian rub, combine in a separate bowl and mix together:

- ¹/₃ **cup toasted sesame oil**
- ¹/₄ **cup minced fresh ginger**
- 3 **tablespoons minced garlic**
- 2 **tablespoons freshly cracked white or black pepper**
- 3 **tablespoons orange zest**
- 3 **tablespoons crushed Szechuan peppers or dried red pepper flakes**

## GRILL

Follow the recipe for Super-Basic Smoke-Roasted Whole Chickens (see page 134) but rub the chickens with the Asian rub after the salt and pepper.

## TOP

When the chickens are rested, carve each chicken into 6 pieces, drizzle with some of the sauce, and serve the rest in a bowl for dipping.

*Curve Ball*

# GARLIC and HERB-RUBBED SMOKE-ROASTED WHOLE CHICKENS with BURNT RED PEPPER COULIS

*WE LIKE nothing better than burning things on purpose; there's just something liberating about it. So we are fans of fire-roasted red peppers like the ones used here. If you've never made them, you're definitely going to like them.*

### PREP

While the fire heats up, combine in a large bowl and mix well:

**1/4 cup extra-virgin olive oil**
**1/4 cup minced fresh garlic**
**1/2 cup chopped fresh herbs, any combination of basil, oregano, thyme, parsley, sage, and/or marjoram**

### GRILL

When the fire is ready, put on the grill right above the coals:

**3 red bell peppers**

Grill the peppers, moving them around with your tongs until all sides are uniformly black and charred. Remove them from the grill and place in a paper bag or aluminum foil for 20 minutes. Peel off the charred skins, slice, deseed, and, to make the coulis, puree in a blender or food processor along with:

**3 cloves garlic, peeled**
**1/4 cup extra-virgin olive oil**
**1/4 cup balsamic vinegar**
**Kosher salt and freshly cracked black pepper to taste**

Now add a couple of handfuls of charcoal to the fire, wait about 10 minutes, and go on to step 2 of the Super-Basic Smoke-Roasted Whole Chickens (see page 134) but rub the chickens with the olive oil–fresh herb mixture after the salt and pepper.

### TOP

When the chickens are ready to go, carve each chicken into 6 pieces, spread out the coulis on a platter, and lay the chicken pieces on top of it. (Or you can just top each piece with a smear of the coulis and serve the rest in a separate bowl for dipping.)

SHRIMP & FISH

# SHRIMP

**WITH THE EXCEPTION OF CANNED TUNA**, shrimp is by far the most-eaten seafood in America. That's okay with us, because it's tasty and easy to cook, and easily adapts to flavor footprints from all over the world—plus it's particularly good with a little char from the grill. It's good to pay a bit of attention, though, to what kind of shrimp you buy. Sometimes down in Costa Rica, when we've been able to track down the fish truck that makes deliveries a couple of times a week at local restaurants, we've gotten our hands on fresh local shrimp. If you can ever do this, don't miss the opportunity: the flavor is amazing—and we don't use that word often. But in most of this country, it's pretty much impossible to buy fresh shrimp. So we suggest you buy frozen rather than the "fresh" shrimp at the fish counter, which is basically just frozen that has been defrosted. That way, you can defrost it right before you're ready to cook it. We like to use large shrimp—which is the term for shrimp that are about 16 to 20 per pound—because they're big enough to be easily handled on the grill but small enough so they're readily available. If you want to go to bigger shrimp (extra-large, which are fewer than 12 per pound), just use the same amount by weight in these recipes. Two other decisions to make when cooking shrimp are whether to remove the shell and whether to devein them. We used to recommend grilling shrimp with the shell on, but in fact that makes it more of a pain to eat—once the shells are cooked, they can be hard to get off. So now we recommend removing the shells before the shrimp goes over the coals. If you prefer to cook the shrimp shell-on because you like the process of prying off the shells and getting your fingers nice and oily, go right ahead—just leave them on the fire slightly longer. Similarly, we now devein shrimp just because we think it gives it a little purer flavor, but this is up to you, too; it certainly isn't unhealthy to leave the vein in. Shrimp cooks quickly, so we recommend that you check early and often for doneness, because overcooked shrimp gets dry and mealy. Finally, since even people who don't like most seafood are good with shrimp, we're giving you an extra recipe or two here.

# Super-Basic
# GRILLED SHRIMP

# Super-Basic
# GRILLED SHRIMP

**2 pounds large shrimp (16/20 per pound) peeled and deveined, tails left on**

**3 tablespoons olive oil**

**Kosher salt and freshly cracked black pepper to taste**

 Build a two-level fire in your grill, which means you put all the coals on one side of the grill and leave the other side free of coals. When the flames have died down, all the coals are covered with gray ash, and the temperature is medium-hot (you can hold your hand 6 inches above the grill for 3 to 4 seconds), you're ready to cook.

Thread the shrimp onto skewers, about 6 per skewer. Drizzle the shrimp with the olive oil and sprinkle them generously with the salt and pepper, then place them on the grill directly over the coals and cook until slightly charred and golden brown, about 3 to 4 minutes per side. To check for doneness, cut into one of the shrimp at its thickest point and peek inside to be sure it is opaque throughout. Serve hot.

---

**Serves 8 as an appetizer, 4 as an entrée**

# GRILLED SHRIMP with NEW ORLEANS-STYLE BARBECUE SAUCE

*THIS ONE is mildly spicy, is very messy, and makes a great appetizer for a big crowd, as long as you provide plenty of paper towels. This also makes a perfect filling for a po'boy, the iconic sandwich of New Orleans, whether "dressed" or "plain."*

**1 →**

**PREP**
While the fire heats up, combine in a small saucepan over low heat:

**1 stick butter**
**1 tablespoon spicy brown mustard**
**3 tablespoons Tabasco sauce**
**2 tablespoons Worcestershire sauce**
**1 tablespoon minced garlic**
**1 tablespoon paprika**

Cook, stirring frequently, until the butter has melted and the ingredients are well blended, then set aside.

**2 →**

**GRILL**
Follow the recipe for Super-Basic Grilled Shrimp on page 147.

**TOSS**

When the shrimp come off the grill, slide them off the skewers into a large bowl. Add the barbecue sauce and toss vigorously to coat.

# CHESAPEAKE BAY-STYLE GRILLED SHRIMP with OLD BAY, LEMON, and BUTTER

*INVENTED back in 1939, Old Bay is a classic spice mixture of the Eastern Shore. We always have it in the pantry, and love it with seafood of any kind.*

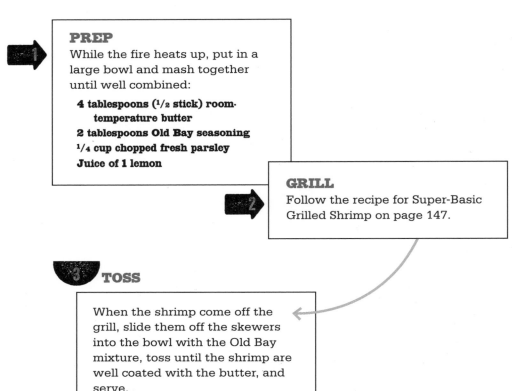

**PREP**
While the fire heats up, put in a large bowl and mash together until well combined:

**4 tablespoons (¹/₂ stick) room-temperature butter**
**2 tablespoons Old Bay seasoning**
**¹/₄ cup chopped fresh parsley**
**Juice of 1 lemon**

**GRILL**
Follow the recipe for Super-Basic Grilled Shrimp on page 147.

**TOSS**
When the shrimp come off the grill, slide them off the skewers into the bowl with the Old Bay mixture, toss until the shrimp are well coated with the butter, and serve.

# JAPANESE-STYLE GRILLED SHRIMP with TOGARASHI

*TOGARASHI, a Japanese seasoning mix also called "7 spice powder," tastes kind of like dashi with lime and kumquat. Chris likes to use it because lots of people have never heard of it and it sounds pretty weird.*

**1**

## PREP
While the fire heats up, place in small individual containers:

- **¹/₃ cup soy sauce**
- **¹/₄ cup mirin**
- **2 tablespoons fresh lime juice (from 1 lime)**
- **2 tablespoons sesame oil**
- **2 tablespoons minced fresh ginger**

**2**

## GRILL
Follow the recipe for Super-Basic Grilled Shrimp on page 147.

**3** TOSS

When the shrimp come off the grill, slide them off the skewers into a large bowl. Add all of the other ingredients one after the other, toss with some attitude, and then sprinkle with:

- **¹/₄ cup finely sliced scallions, white and light green parts**
- **3 tablespoons togarashi powder**

# THAI-STYLE GRILLED SHRIMP with TOMATO, GINGER, and LIME

*THE CLASSIC THAI approach featuring sweet, sour, spicy, and hot all at once. Dial up the heat with additional chile peppers of your choice.*

## PREP

While the fire heats up, set out in small individual containers:

**1 medium tomato, diced medium**

**1 peeled, seeded, and diced cucumber**

**3 tablespoons minced fresh ginger**

**1/4 cup roughly chopped fresh mint**

**1/4 cup roughly chopped fresh basil**

**1/4 cup roughly chopped fresh cilantro**

**1/4 cup fish sauce**

**1/4 cup fresh lime juice (from 2 limes)**

**2 tablespoons sugar**

**2 tablespoons chopped fresh chiles of your choice**

## GRILL

Follow the recipe for Super-Basic Grilled Shrimp on page 147.

## TOSS

When the shrimp come off the grill, slide them off the skewers into a large bowl. Sequentially dump in each of the other ingredients and toss, toss, toss.

# CUMIN SEED-CRUSTED GRILLED SHRIMP with CHARRED CORN VINAIGRETTE

*YOU DON'T NEED to cook the corn through here; you just want to give it a little flavorful smoky char.*

## PREP

While the fire heats up, whisk together thoroughly in a large bowl:

- 1/3 cup extra-virgin olive oil
- 1/4 cup fresh lime juice (from 2 limes)
- 1/4 cup roughly chopped fresh cilantro
- 2 tablespoons chili powder
- Kosher salt and freshly cracked black pepper to taste

## GRILL

When the fire is ready, put on the grill right above the coals:

- 2 ears corn, husked

Grill the corn, moving it around with your tongs so all sides get exposed to the heat, just until it's slightly charred, about 2 minutes total. Then remove from the grill, slice the kernels off the cob, and add them to the large bowl.

Now follow step 2 of Super-Basic Grilled Shrimp (see page 147). Just before the shrimp go on the grill, though, press onto them so that they adhere:

- 2 tablespoons cumin seeds

## TOSS

When the shrimp come off the grill, add them to the bowl with the corn vinaigrette, toss, and serve.

# GRILLED SHRIMP TACOS with AVOCADO and GRILLED PINEAPPLE

*TACOS A LA PLAtA: Born on the beach in Costa Rica, this is among our very favorite lunch dishes. Vamos, amigos!*

## PREP

While the fire heats up, combine in a large bowl:

**1 cup shredded cabbage**
**2 avocados, diced medium**

Next, place in separate small containers:

**¹/₄ cup extra-virgin olive oil**
**¹/₂ cup roughly chopped fresh cilantro leaves**
**1 to 2 tablespoons chopped fresh chiles of your choice**
**1 tablespoon ground cumin**
**¹/₃ cup fresh lime juice (from 2 or 3 limes)**

## GRILL

When the fire is ready, put on the grill right above the coals:

**1 dozen 6-inch corn tortillas**
**3 (1-inch-thick) slices fresh pineapple, peeled and cored**

Grill the tortillas for just 30 seconds per side to heat, then put them aside; grill the pineapple until golden, 4 to 5 minutes per side. When the pineapple comes off the grill, cut it into medium dice and put into the large bowl

Now follow step 2 of the recipe for Super-Basic Grilled Shrimp on page 147.

## TOSS

When the shrimp come off the grill, slide them off the skewers into the bowl with the cabbage mixture, add all the other prepped ingredients, and toss like crazy. Season to taste and serve with the grilled tortillas.

# fish FILLETS

**MOVING UP THE LADDER** of fish grilling from carefree to maddening, fillets are right in the middle—more difficult than steak fish but easier than whole fish. Basically, a fillet is a piece of fish created by slicing lengthwise along one side of the fish parallel to the backbone, so it contains none of the backbone. This makes it more delicate and therefore harder to handle on the grill. If possible, you should get your fillets skin-on, since this helps hold them together; it's easy to remove the skin after they're cooked. As with fish steaks, there are a few things you can do to decrease your chances of sticking. Here's the drill: Make sure the grill grid is very clean, then put it over the coals and let it get good and hot before you put on your fillets. If you're applying oil to the fish, do so very lightly so you don't get a flare-up when the fish goes onto the grill. And when you do put the fish onto the grill, don't move it for at least two minutes—you want the fish to develop a nice, firm crust, which will cause it to release from the grill grid much more easily. Obviously, fillets come in different sizes, but we've given general directions here and cook over a medium fire, which gives you more room for error. But the cooking times are, even more than usual, an estimate, and you should check your fillets early and often for doneness, since those signs are going to be more reliable here. Checking for doneness is easy enough—just slip a thin-bladed knife into the thickest part of the fillet and take a peek at the center. What you are looking for is that moment when the center just turns from translucent to opaque. As for manipulating the fillets—putting them on the grill, flipping them, and removing them—we favor tongs, as for almost every other grilling task. However, it's also a good idea to have one of those thin-bladed fish spatulas around, which are useful for sliding under a fillet to remove it if it has, by some odd chance, stuck to the grill.

# Super-Basic
# GRILLED FISH FILLETS

# Super-Basic
# GRILLED FISH FILLETS

4 fillets of fish, such as salmon, mahimahi, bluefish, or halibut, 6 to 8 ounces each

2 tablespoons olive oil

Kosher salt and freshly cracked black pepper to taste

 Build a two-level fire in your grill, which means you put all the coals on one side of the grill and leave the other side free of coals. When the flames have died down, all the coals are covered with gray ash, and the temperature is medium (you can hold your hand 6 inches above the grill for 4 to 5 seconds), you're ready to cook.

 Rub the fillets on both sides with olive oil and sprinkle them generously with the salt and pepper. Put the fillets on the grill directly over the coals and cook, turning once, until they are cooked through, about 6 to 8 minutes per side. To check for doneness, make a small cut in the thickest part of one of the fillets and peek in to be sure it is just opaque all the way through.

Serves 8 as an appetizer, 4 as an entrée

# GRILLED FISH FILLETS with OLD BAY TARTAR SAUCE

*THERE'S A LONGSTANDING relationship between Old Bay, tartar sauce, and fish, and we're happy to keep that relationship going. And by the way—it's incredibly easy to make your own mayo (page 232); if you've got 10 minutes, do it.*

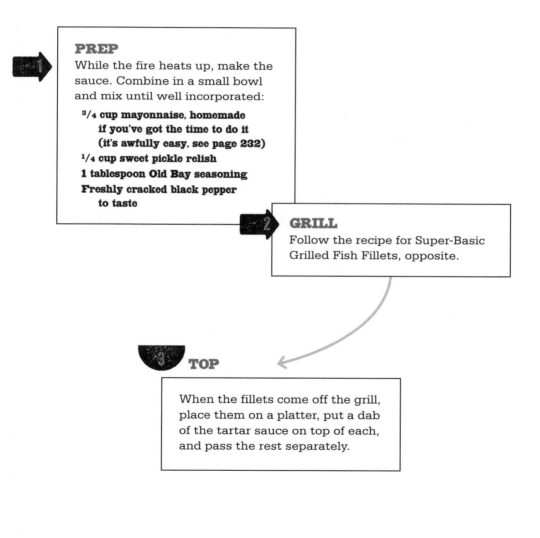

**1**

### PREP
While the fire heats up, make the sauce. Combine in a small bowl and mix until well incorporated:

**³/₄ cup mayonnaise, homemade if you've got the time to do it (it's awfully easy, see page 232)**
**¹/₄ cup sweet pickle relish**
**1 tablespoon Old Bay seasoning**
**Freshly cracked black pepper to taste**

**2**

### GRILL
Follow the recipe for Super-Basic Grilled Fish Fillets, opposite.

**3**

### TOP
When the fillets come off the grill, place them on a platter, put a dab of the tartar sauce on top of each, and pass the rest separately.

# GRILLED FISH FILLETS with TABASCO REMOULADE

*HERE'S ANOTHER EXAMPLE of the fact that spicy and seafood are actually a good match when you do it right.*

**1** → **PREP**

While the fire heats up, make the remoulade. Combine in a small bowl until well incorporated:

- 3/4 cup mayonnaise, preferably home-made if you're feelin' it (it's easy, see page 232)
- 2 tablespoons capers
- 1/4 cup roughly chopped fresh parsley
- 2 tablespoons coarse-ground mustard
- 2 tablespoons Tabasco sauce (or less if you're a wimp)
- 1 teaspoon ground white or freshly cracked black pepper
- Kosher salt to taste (if needed)

**GRILL**

Follow the recipe for Super-Basic Grilled Fish Fillets on page 158.

 **TOP**

When the fillets come off the grill, place them on a platter, put a dab of the remoulade on top of each, and pass the rest separately.

# GRILLED FISH FILLETS with SIMPLE GREEN SAUCE

*CLOSE YOUR EYES when you're eating this, and you might think you're in the south of France. Or maybe not, but we think you'll be happy. This is best with lighter fish such as halibut or striped bass.*

**PREP**

While the fire heats up, chop and measure the following, keeping each in a separate small container:

- **1/2 cup roughly chopped fresh flat-leaf parsley**
- **1/2 cup extra-virgin olive oil**
- **1 tablespoon red wine vinegar**
- **2 tablespoons capers**
- **1 tablespoon minced anchovies (optional)**
- **Kosher salt and freshly cracked black pepper to taste**

**GRILL**

Follow the recipe for Super-Basic Grilled Fish Fillets on page 158.

**TOP**

When the fillets come off the grill, put them on a platter or individual plates and drizzle heavily with the green sauce. If you've got sauce left, pass it separately.

# GRILLED FISH FILLETS with COMPLEX GREEN SAUCE

*THIS ONE is better with your more full-flavored (that is, fattier) fish, such as bluefish or salmon.*

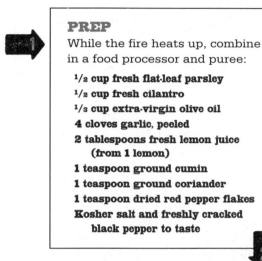

**PREP**

While the fire heats up, combine in a food processor and puree:

- **1/2 cup fresh flat-leaf parsley**
- **1/2 cup fresh cilantro**
- **1/3 cup extra-virgin olive oil**
- **4 cloves garlic, peeled**
- **2 tablespoons fresh lemon juice (from 1 lemon)**
- **1 teaspoon ground cumin**
- **1 teaspoon ground coriander**
- **1 teaspoon dried red pepper flakes**
- **Kosher salt and freshly cracked black pepper to taste**

**GRILL**

Follow the recipe for Super-Basic Grilled Fish Fillets on page 158.

 **TOP**

When the fillets come off the grill, put them on a platter or individual plates, put a swipe of the green sauce on top of each, and pass the rest of the sauce separately. (If you happen to have any sauce left over, toss it with enough pasta for one person.)

# GRILLED FISH FILLETS with ANCHO CHILE SALSA

*YOU CAN SUBSTITUTE two tablespoons of chili powder for the dried chile here, but anchos are pretty easy to find these days, and their mild heat and fruity flavor are an excellent match with the fish.*

**PREP**

While the fire heats up, combine and puree in a blender or food processor:

    **2 ancho chiles (or any medium-hot dried red chiles such as pasilla, New Mexico, or mulato)**
    **2 tablespoons extra-virgin olive oil**

Then put them in a small bowl and mix together with:

    **2 tablespoons extra-virgin olive oil**
    **¼ cup small-diced red onion**
    **¼ cup roughly chopped fresh cilantro**
    **¼ cup fresh lime juice (from 2 limes)**
    **1 teaspoon ground cumin**

**GRILL**

Follow the recipe for Super-Basic Grilled Fish Fillets on page 158.

 **TOP**

When the fillets come off the grill, put them on a platter or individual plates, top with a bit of the chile salsa, and serve the rest separately.

# GRILLED FISH FILLETS with THAI-STYLE SESAME VINAIGRETTE

*THIS VERSATILE VINAIGRETTE, another vindication of the Southeast Asian tradition of jazzy flavors with seafood, works well with either strong-flavored or mild fish.*

**PREP**

While the fire heats up, combine in a small bowl and mix until well incorporated:

¹/₄ cup toasted sesame oil

¹/₄ cup fresh lime juice (from 2 limes)

2 tablespoons fish sauce

1 tablespoon minced fresh ginger

1 teaspoon minced fresh garlic

1 tablespoon minced chiles of your choice

1 tablespoon sugar

Kosher salt and freshly cracked black pepper to taste

**GRILL**

Follow the recipe for Super-Basic Grilled Fish Fillets on page 158.

**3 TOP**

When the fillets come off the grill, put them on platters or serve one to each person, then drizzle heavily with the vinaigrette.

*Curve Ball*

# GRILLED FISH FILLETS with ASIAN SAUSAGE RELISH

WE BELIEVE that everything goes better with a little pork, and that includes sea-food. Asian and Portuguese cooks seem to agree with us, so we're not alone here.

## PREP
While the fire heats up, remove the casings and sauté over medium heat until slightly browned and crumbly, about 6 to 8 minutes, then drain off almost all of its fat and cool to room temperature:

**8 ounces fresh pork sausage (Italian or spicy is fine, as is straight-up ground pork)**

When the sausage has cooled to room temperature, add and mix together well:

**3 tablespoons minced ginger**
**1 tablespoon minced garlic**
**1 tablespoon minced fresh chiles of your choice**
**2 tablespoons soy sauce**
**1 teaspoon sugar**
**1/4 cup minced scallions, white and light green parts**
**Kosher salt and ground white or freshly cracked black pepper to taste**

## GRILL
Follow the recipe for Super-Basic Grilled Fish Fillets on page 158.

## TOP
When the fillets come off the grill, put them on a platter, and top with the warm relish.

# tuna STEAKS

**WHEN CHRIS OPENED** the East Coast Grill way back in 1985, tuna that was grilled to crusty on the outside but dead rare on the inside was on the menu. In those days, it was considered cutting edge, slightly outrageous, almost dangerous; now it's de rigueur in restaurants all over the country. But it hasn't become any less delicious over the intervening years. To our minds, tuna is the archetypal grilling fish—sturdy, as easy to cook as beefsteak (and best cooked to the same degree, in our opinion), with that smooth, clear, fresh, indescribable flavor. Plus it takes perfectly to the well-seared-outside, rare-inside dynamic that a hot live fire is uniquely able to create. Two things about your tuna steaks are particularly important here: First, make sure they are about two inches thick, so the center stays almost raw while the outside gets nicely seared. And second, make sure they are superfresh. The best way to ensure this is to find a fishmonger who you get to know and trust. If you don't have a relationship with the person who sells you the fish, ask to smell it; if it smells like fish, don't even consider using it this way. You can still use it, but you will need to cook it all the way through. There are lots of ways to prepare grilled tuna, but here we are going to break with our usual MO and basically give you a batch of dishes with Asian flavors, because we think that's what works best with tuna. You can, of course, also use the Super-Basic Grilled Tuna Steaks method with other flavor profiles, but in that case use a more neutral oil and skip the white pepper.

# Super-Basic
# GRILLED TUNA STEAKS

170

with **Soy** and **Wasabi**

171

with **Sweet and Sour Chile-Garlic Glaze**

173

with **Szechuan Black Bean Sauce**

174

with **Soy, Mustard,** and **Honey**

175

with **Sesame-Seaweed Salad**

176

with **Homemade Teriyaki Sauce**

178

with **Korean-Style Cucumber-Sprout Relish**

179

# Super-Basic
# GRILLED TUNA STEAKS

**4 (2-inch-thick) tuna steaks, about 8 ounces each**
**3 tablespoons sesame oil**
**Kosher salt and freshly cracked black pepper to taste**
**1/4 cup freshly cracked white pepper**

 Build a two-level fire in your grill, which means you put all the coals on one side of the grill and leave the other side free of coals. When the flames have died down, all the coals are covered with gray ash, and the temperature is hot (you can hold your hand 6 inches above the coals for only 2 to 3 seconds), you're ready to cook.

 Rub the tuna steaks all over with the sesame oil and sprinkle them generously with the salt and peppers, then pat gently to be sure the peppers and salt adhere.

 Place the tuna steaks on the grill directly over the coals and cook until well seared on both sides and done the way you like them, about 4 to 5 minutes total for medium rare, 6 to 8 minutes if you want your tuna cooked all the way through. To check for doneness, cut into one of the pieces of tuna and see if it is just slightly less done than you want it to be when you eat it. (The fish will continue to cook a bit after being removed from the grill.) Remove the tuna steaks from the grill and serve warm.

**Serves 4**

# GRILLED TUNA STEAKS with SOY and WASABI

*WELL, no surprise that this archetypal sushi flavor combination is perfectly great with rare tuna, too.*

**PREP**

While the fire heats up, combine in a medium bowl and mix until a paste forms:

**1 tablespoon wasabi powder**
**1 tablespoon water**

Mix into the paste until well combined:

**¹/₂ cup soy sauce**
**2 tablespoons minced pickled ginger**
**   or minced raw ginger**

**GRILL**

Follow the recipe for Super-Basic Grilled Tuna Steaks, opposite.

 **TOP**

When the tuna steaks come off the grill, put them on a platter, spoon a bit of the sauce over each, and pass the rest for dipping.

# GRILLED TUNA STEAKS with SWEET AND SOUR CHILE-GARLIC GLAZE

*SWEET AND SOUR TUNA? Well, yes, kind of. It may sound hokey, but it's awfully good.*

### PREP

While the fire heats up, combine in a small saucepan over medium heat and cook, stirring frequently, until the preserves are melted, which should take about 5 minutes:

**¹/₂ cup apricot preserves**
**¹/₄ cup rice wine vinegar**

Remove the glaze from the heat and stir in:

**¹/₃ cup chile-garlic sambal**

### GRILL

Follow the recipe for Super-Basic Grilled Tuna Steaks (see page 170), but during the last 60 seconds of cooking, brush the tuna steaks with the glaze, the flip them and brush the second side with the glaze, too.

### TOP

When the tuna steaks come off the grill, put them on a platter, give each another swipe of the glaze, then sprinkle with:

**¹/₃ cup chopped scallions, white and light green parts**

Serve, passing the rest of the glaze as a dipping sauce.

# GRILLED TUNA STEAKS with SZECHUAN BLACK BEAN SAUCE

*FRAGRANT Szechuan peppers have a distinctive woody, lemonlike flavor. Plus, if you use enough of them—which we do here—they make your mouth numb.*

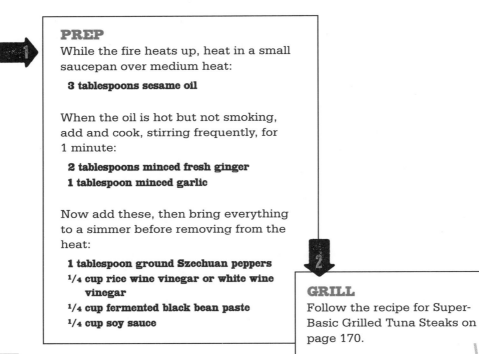

**PREP**

While the fire heats up, heat in a small saucepan over medium heat:

**3 tablespoons sesame oil**

When the oil is hot but not smoking, add and cook, stirring frequently, for 1 minute:

**2 tablespoons minced fresh ginger**
**1 tablespoon minced garlic**

Now add these, then bring everything to a simmer before removing from the heat:

**1 tablespoon ground Szechuan peppers**
**¼ cup rice wine vinegar or white wine vinegar**
**¼ cup fermented black bean paste**
**¼ cup soy sauce**

**GRILL**

Follow the recipe for Super-Basic Grilled Tuna Steaks on page 170.

**TOP**

When the tuna steaks come off the grill, put them on a platter or individual plates, top each steak with a generous amount of the black bean sauce and then sprinkle the tuna steaks with:

**¼ cup chopped fresh cilantro**

Pass the remaining sauce for dipping. If you've got any left over, stir it into egg noodles for a little Asian snack.

# GRILLED TUNA STEAKS with SOY, MUSTARD, and HONEY

*TO US, cardamom always brings a whiff of the exotic. Superfloral, highly aromatic and citrusy, with a nice bit of astringency to prevent those things from getting out of hand, it's a great spice to get to know.*

### PREP
While the fire heats, combine in a medium bowl:

**1/2 cup soy sauce**
**2 tablespoons powdered mustard**

Mix into the soy sauce and mustard until well combined:

**2 tablespoons honey**
**2 ground green cardamom seeds**

### GRILL
Follow the recipe for Super-Basic Grilled Tuna Steaks on page 170.

 ### TOP

When the tuna steaks come off the grill, put them on a platter or individual plates, smear each one with a tablespoon or so of the sauce, and pass the rest in a bowl for dipping.

# GRILLED TUNA STEAKS with SESAME-SEAWEED SALAD

SEAWEED has a kind of bad name in the United States, largely from its health food days back in the 1960s. These days, though, there are many kinds available, and they're all very tasty when used right—vegetal in a pleasant way, slightly salty, refreshing. And, of course, they are particularly nice paired with their fellow water creatures, as we do here.

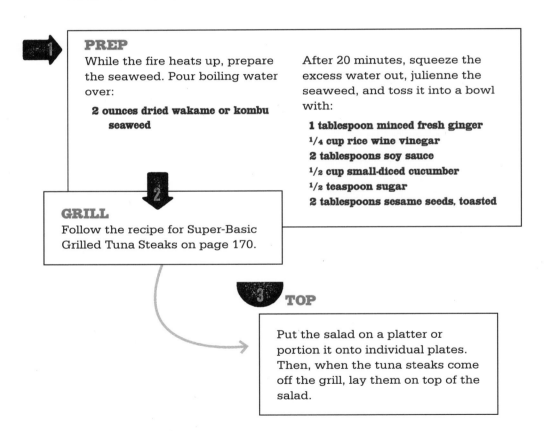

**1 PREP**

While the fire heats up, prepare the seaweed. Pour boiling water over:

**2 ounces dried wakame or kombu seaweed**

After 20 minutes, squeeze the excess water out, julienne the seaweed, and toss it into a bowl with:

**1 tablespoon minced fresh ginger**
**¼ cup rice wine vinegar**
**2 tablespoons soy sauce**
**½ cup small-diced cucumber**
**½ teaspoon sugar**
**2 tablespoons sesame seeds, toasted**

**2 GRILL**

Follow the recipe for Super-Basic Grilled Tuna Steaks on page 170.

**3 TOP**

Put the salad on a platter or portion it onto individual plates. Then, when the tuna steaks come off the grill, lay them on top of the salad.

# GRILLED TUNA STEAKS with HOMEMADE TERIYAKI SAUCE

*LIKE MOST of the stuff we tend to buy premade (ketchup, mustard, mayonnaise, and so on), teriyaki sauce is better when you make it yourself. Plus you can make it really spicy. (It is also excellent on steak.)*

**PREP**

While the fire heats up, combine in a small saucepan over low heat and cook, stirring occasionally, for 15 to 20 minutes until the mixture is slightly tacky and kind of syrupy:

- ½ cup soy sauce
- ½ cup mirin
- ½ cup dry sherry
- 2 tablespoons minced fresh ginger

Remove the sauce from the heat and stir in:

- ⅓ cup chile-garlic sambal

**GRILL**

Follow the recipe for Super-Basic Grilled Tuna Steaks (see page 170), brushing the steaks with the teriyaki sauce on both sides during the last 60 seconds of cooking.

**TOP**

When the tuna steaks come off the grill, brush each with another thin layer of the sauce, put the rest of the sauce in a dish to pass for dipping, and sprinkle the steaks evenly with:

- ¼ cup chopped scallions, white and light green parts
- ¼ cup toasted sesame seeds
- 1 tablespoon ground Szechuan chiles

*Curve Ball*

# GRILLED TUNA STEAKS with
# KOREAN-STYLE CUCUMBER-SPROUT RELISH

*THIS RELISH is a sort of fresh kimchi. The gochugaru is pretty essential, so get your hands on some if you're going to make this recipe. If you're like Doc, you will leave out the bean sprouts; if you're like Chris, you'll use extra.*

**PREP**

While the fire heats up, combine in a large bowl and mix well:

<sup></sup>1/2 **cup peeled, seeded, and small-diced cucumber**

1/2 **cup mung or other bean sprouts**

1 **teaspoon minced garlic**

1/4 **cup rice wine vinegar or white wine vinegar**

2 **tablespoons soy sauce**

1 **tablespoon fish sauce**

1 **tablespoon gochugaru (Korean red pepper powder)**

**GRILL**

Follow the recipe for Super-Basic Grilled Tuna Steaks on page 170.

**TOP**

When the tuna steaks come off the grill, put them on a platter or individual plates, top each one with some of the relish, and then sprinkle with:

1/4 **cup toasted sesame seeds**

1/4 **cup toasted nori**

1/4 **cup minced scallions, white and light green parts**

# other fish STEAKS

**AS WITH MEAT, SO WITH FISH:** we prefer anything that has a bone in it. When fish is made into steaks, it is cut perpendicular to the spine, as opposed to fillets, which are cut parallel to the spine. In most cases this means that fish steaks come bone-in. That not only makes them more flavorful, but also gives them more structure, which translates into being easier to handle on the grill. Easier to cook and better flavor—doesn't that seem like a combination that's worth exploring? Most any fillet fish can be cut into steaks. Salmon is a great example of a fish that you see often in both fillet form and steak form; obviously, we'd recommend you go for the steak option. We've also had some success in cutting both striped bass and bluefish into steaks, and in Costa Rica we've seen mahimahi cut into steaks. You can ask your fishmonger if, when cutting up whole fish, he or she can cut some into steaks for you instead of fillets. This will impress the fishmonger (which is good because he or she will be more likely to steer you to the best and freshest fish the next time you come in). Or you can just ask the fishmonger what fish is available in steak form that day—the choices are most likely to be along the lines of swordfish, halibut, cod, grouper, or salmon, as well as tuna (see pages 170 through 179 for our tuna recipes). Either way, whether you ask for special treatment or select from what your fishmonger already has, you're very likely to end up with a better dinner. As always when cooking fish, make sure your grill grid is superclean. Let the grid heat up for a while before you put the fish on, and then let the fish sit for a couple of minutes before you even think about moving it—the heat will create a sear on the surface of the fish that will make it much easier to move. As you will see from the recipes in this section, we like fish steaks with compound butters, which are also a standard with beefsteak.

# Super-Basic
# GRILLED FISH STEAKS

182

with **Orange-Chipotle Butter**

183

with **Sriracha-Basil Butter**

184

with **Green Olive–Sun-Dried Tomato Relish**

185

with **Spicy Yogurt-Cucumber Sauce**

186

with **Walnut-Pomegranate Mixture**

187

**Grilled Coriander-Crusted Fish Steaks**
with **Gazpacho Relish**

188

# Super-Basic
# GRILLED FISH STEAKS

4 (1-inch-thick) fish steaks, such as swordfish, tuna, halibut,
or salmon, each 8 to 10 ounces
3 tablespoons olive oil
Kosher salt and freshly cracked black pepper to taste

 Build a two-level fire in your grill, which means you put all the coals on one side of the grill and leave the other side free of coals. When the flames have died down, all the coals are covered with gray ash, and the temperature is hot (you can hold your hand 6 inches above the grill for only 2 to 3 seconds), you're ready to cook.

 Rub the steaks with the oil and sprinkle them generously with the salt and pepper, pressing gently to make sure the seasoning adheres to the fish. Place the fish on the grill directly over the coals and cook until the interior is just opaque throughout, about 5 to 6 minutes per side. To check for doneness, cut into one of the steaks and peek to be sure it is just opaque throughout. Serve hot.

 | Serves 4 |

# GRILLED FISH STEAKS with ORANGE-CHIPOTLE BUTTER

*THE COMINGLING of the smoky chipotle flavor with the char of the grill has always been one of our favorite combinations.*

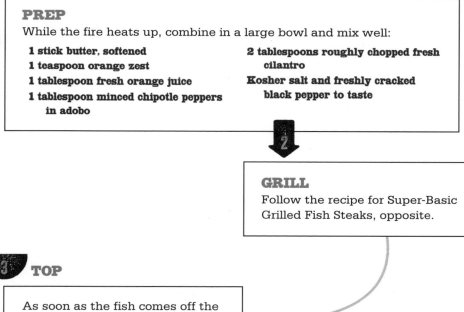

**PREP**
While the fire heats up, combine in a large bowl and mix well:

- **1 stick butter, softened**
- **1 teaspoon orange zest**
- **1 tablespoon fresh orange juice**
- **1 tablespoon minced chipotle peppers in adobo**

- **2 tablespoons roughly chopped fresh cilantro**
- **Kosher salt and freshly cracked black pepper to taste**

**GRILL**
Follow the recipe for Super-Basic Grilled Fish Steaks, opposite.

**TOP**

As soon as the fish comes off the grill (don't wait), top each steak with a couple tablespoons of the orange-chipotle butter and serve right away.

# GRILLED FISH STEAKS with SRIRACHA-BASIL BUTTER

*SRIRACHA is not just one of our favorite ingredients; it's also insanely popular with cooks all over the country, and for good reason. Plus, it likes fish.*

### PREP
While the fire heats up, combine in a large bowl and mix well:

- **1 stick butter, softened**
- **2 tablespoons Sriracha (or less if you like milder food)**
- **1 tablespoon minced fresh ginger**
- **2 tablespoons minced fresh Thai or Italian basil**
- **Kosher salt and freshly cracked black pepper to taste**

### GRILL
Follow the recipe for Super-Basic Grilled Fish Steaks on page 182.

### TOP
Right when the fish comes off the grill, top each steak with a tablespoon of the Sriracha butter.

# GRILLED FISH STEAKS with
# GREEN OLIVE–SUN-DRIED TOMATO RELISH

*WE KNOW that not everybody loves sun-dried tomatoes, but to us they taste a little like bacon, and what could be better than that? But if you don't agree, you can always substitute fresh tomatoes here.*

### PREP
While the fire heats up, combine in a large bowl and mix well:

- $1/3$ **cup good-quality green olives, pitted and diced small**
- $1/3$ **cup minced sun-dried tomatoes**
- $1/4$ **cup extra-virgin olive oil**
- **1 teaspoon minced garlic**
- **2 tablespoons roughly chopped fresh marjoram or oregano**

### GRILL
Follow the recipe for Super-Basic Grilled Fish Steaks on page 182.

### TOP
When the fish is done, top each steak with some of the relish and pass any left over in a small bowl.

# GRILLED FISH STEAKS with
# SPICY YOGURT-CUCUMBER SAUCE

THIS IS our take on the classic Middle Eastern sauce—though in Turkey you would likely be ostracized if you served yogurt with fish.

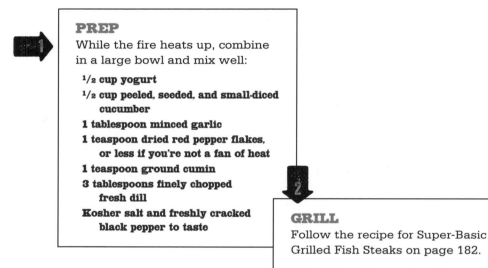

**1** **PREP**

While the fire heats up, combine in a large bowl and mix well:

- ¹/₂ **cup yogurt**
- ¹/₂ **cup peeled, seeded, and small-diced cucumber**
- **1 tablespoon minced garlic**
- **1 teaspoon dried red pepper flakes, or less if you're not a fan of heat**
- **1 teaspoon ground cumin**
- **3 tablespoons finely chopped fresh dill**
- **Kosher salt and freshly cracked black pepper to taste**

**2** **GRILL**

Follow the recipe for Super-Basic Grilled Fish Steaks on page 182.

 **TOP**

When the fish comes off the grill, top each steak with some of the sauce and, if you want, sprinkle evenly with:

- **1 tablespoon sumac**

# GRILLED FISH STEAKS with
# WALNUT-POMEGRANATE MIXTURE

*WE'RE STAYING in the Middle East for this one—pomegranate molasses and walnuts are a classic combination. If you don't have pomegranate molasses (though you should), you can use pomegranate seeds.*

### PREP
While the fire heats up, combine in a large bowl and mix well:

¹/₂ cup toasted walnuts, coarsely chopped

1 tablespoon minced garlic

2 tablespoons pomegranate molasses or ¹/₄ cup pomegranate seeds

¹/₄ cup roughly chopped fresh cilantro

1 teaspoon ground cumin

Kosher salt and freshly cracked black pepper to taste

### GRILL
Follow the recipe for Super-Basic Grilled Fish Steaks on page 182.

 **TOP**

When the fish comes off the grill, top the steaks with some of the relish and pass the rest separately. (If there's any left over after you eat, save it and mix it with rice.)

# GRILLED CORIANDER-CRUSTED FISH STEAKS with GAZPACHO RELISH

*YOU MIGHT want to serve this in a shallow soup bowl— the relish is pretty liquid-y, somewhere between a relish and real gazpacho.*

## PREP

While the fire heats up, combine in a large bowl and mix well:

1 cup Clamato juice

⅓ cup peeled, seeded, and small-diced cucumber

⅓ cup small-diced red pepper

⅓ cup small-diced celery

¼ cup red wine vinegar

¼ cup extra-virgin olive oil

Kosher salt and freshly cracked black pepper to taste

## GRILL

Follow the recipe for Super-Basic Grilled Fish Steaks (see page 182) and add to the salt and pepper rub:

2 tablespoons roughly cracked coriander seeds

 **TOP**

When the fish comes off the grill, top each steak with some of the relish, then sprinkle with:

¼ cup chopped fresh flat-leaf parsley

¼ cup dried bread crumbs (homemade are best)

1 tablespoon lemon zest

VEGETABLES

# VEGETABLES
## love the grill, too

**WE CAN STILL REMEMBER** the bad old days when most Americans considered it rather strange to grill vegetables: the only proper option for the grill was meat—and primarily hot dogs, steaks, and burgers, at that. Fortunately, that has all changed, and vegetables have come into their own as grilling fare. Yet for recipe inspiration, we still tend to look to the cuisines of countries where fire and vegetables have a longstanding relationship, particularly the Middle East and Italy. Of course, some Asian influences and good old American flavors sneak in there, too. We have certain preferences for how to deal with the various vegetables we've included here. For example, we like to use small new potatoes no bigger than a golf ball and cut them in half. That has several advantages: they cook quite quickly, they don't roll around on the grill, and there is a nice, flat surface that will take on a good sear. When it comes to eggplants, we slice them lengthwise into inch-thick planks, which gives you the best chance of getting them nicely seared on the outside and cooked through on the inside at about the same time. Don't overcook them; they should be just translucent all the way through, but not floppy and mushy. It might help if you think of them as vegetable steaks. As for corn, we have grilled it many ways over the years, but we've ended up preferring to blanch it so that it's about three-quarters cooked, then finish it right over the flames so it gets that toasty, nutty flavor. Cherry tomatoes are too small even for us to want to deal with individually on the grill, so we skewer them. But beware: this is another vegetable you don't want to overcook. You are really only looking to get tomatoes soft and a bit blistered; if you go much further than that, you're going to lose most of the juice. Finally, the thing about asparagus is that it comes in various thicknesses. Any of these recipes will work with any size, but we do think the lighter-flavored recipes match up a bit better with the delicate small asparagus, while those with bolder flavors are nice with the bigger stalks.

# new potatoes

# Super-Basic
# GRILLED NEW POTATOES

**20 golf-ball-size new potatoes, well washed and halved**

**3 tablespoons olive oil**

**Kosher salt and freshly cracked black pepper to taste**

 Build a two-level fire in your grill, which means you put all the coals on one side of the grill and leave the other side free of coals. When the flames have died down, all the coals are covered with gray ash, and the temperature is medium (you can hold your hand 6 inches above the grill for 4 to 5 seconds), you're ready to cook.

Meanwhile, bring a large pan of salted water to a boil on the stovetop, add the potatoes, and cook until they can be easily pierced with a fork but still have some resistance, about 6 to 8 minutes. Immediately plunge them into ice water, then drain and refrigerate them until the fire is ready.

 When the fire is at the right heat, put the potatoes in a large bowl and toss them with the oil, salt, and pepper. Now put them on the grill directly over the coals, cut side down, and cook 5 to 7 minutes, then flip over and cook until nicely browned, 4 to 6 minutes more. Take the potatoes off the grill, put them into a big serving bowl, and let people have at them.

**Serves 4 to 6 as a side dish**

# GRILLED NEW POTATOES with MUSTARD-DILL VINAIGRETTE

*THIS IS quite a vinegary vinaigrette, which we think goes well with the slightly bland flavor of the potatoes. The vinaigrette is also pretty thick, so make sure you toss the potatoes well to get them more or less evenly covered.*

### PREP

While the fire heats up, combine in a large bowl and whisk until well incorporated:

**1/3 cup coarse-ground mustard**
**3 tablespoons extra-virgin olive oil**
**2 tablespoons red wine vinegar**

While gently stirring, add to the bowl:

**1/4 cup finely chopped fresh dill**
**Kosher salt and freshly cracked**
**black pepper to taste**

### GRILL

Follow the recipe for Super-Basic Grilled New Potatoes, opposite.

### TOSS

When the potatoes come off the grill, put them in a large bowl, drizzle the vinaigrette all over them, then toss vigorously; you want the potatoes to all get nicely covered with the vinaigrette.

# GRILLED NEW POTATOES with CORN, BACON, and SAGE

*THIS CLASSIC late-summer combination is equally good hot or cold. You can substitute chives for the sage if you want a brighter flavor here.*

### PREP
While the fire heats up, set out these ingredients in small individual containers:

- 1/4 cup extra-virgin olive oil
- 1/4 cup balsamic vinegar
- 1/2 cup corn kernels (from 1 ear of corn), blanched in boiling salted water for 30 seconds and drained
- 8 slices bacon, cooked until crisp and then crumbled
- 3 tablespoons finely chopped fresh sage
- Kosher salt and freshly cracked black pepper to taste

### GRILL
Follow the recipe for Super-Basic Grilled New Potatoes on page 194.

### TOSS
When the potatoes come off the grill, put them in a large bowl, add all the other ingredients one after another, and toss them with style.

# HOT GRILLED POTATO SALAD

*HERE'S OUR straightforward warm potato salad, but with the added dimension of the slightly smokiness and char from the grill.*

### PREP
While the fire heats up, get all these things ready and set them out in small individual containers:

¼ **cup extra-virgin olive oil**

¼ **cup sherry vinegar**

1 **teaspoon minced garlic**

½ **cup small-diced red pepper**

¼ **cup small-diced celery**

¼ **cup roughly chopped fresh flat-leaf parsley**

1 **teaspoon mustard seed**

1 **teaspoon celery seed**

**Kosher salt and freshly cracked black pepper to taste**

### GRILL
Follow the recipe for Super-Basic Grilled New Potatoes on page 194.

### TOSS
As soon as the potatoes come off the grill, put them in a large bowl, dump in all the other ingredients, toss well, and serve while still warm.

# eggplant

## Super-Basic
## GRILLED EGGPLANT
200

with **Hoisin Sauce, Scallions,** and **Sesame**
201

with **Feta** and **Maras Pepper**
203

**Mediterranean-Style Grilled Eggplant Relish**
204

# Super-Basic
# GRILLED EGGPLANT

1 large or 2 small eggplants, about 2 pounds total, cut lengthwise into
planks about 1 inch thick
1/4 cup olive or vegetable oil
Kosher salt and freshly cracked black pepper to taste

 Build a two-level fire in your grill, which means you put all the coals on one side of the grill and leave the other side free of coals. When the flames have died down, all the coals are covered with gray ash, and the temperature is medium (you can hold your hand 6 inches above the grill for 4 to 5 seconds), you're ready to cook.

 Rub the eggplant planks on both sides with the oil, sprinkle them generously with the salt and pepper, then put them on the grill directly over the coals and cook until golden brown on the outside and translucent all the way through, about 3 to 4 minutes per side. Be careful not to overcook these, and try to maintain some rigidity, since the eggplant should not be floppy when cooked. Remove the eggplant planks from the grill, put them on a platter, and serve 'em.

**Serves 4 as a side dish**

# GRILLED EGGPLANT with
# HOISIN SAUCE, SCALLIONS, and SESAME

*WE LIKE Asian flavors with eggplant —which makes sense, since it's a favored vegetable in that part of the world.*

## PREP
While the fire heats up, combine in a large bowl and mix well:

**¼ cup chopped scallions, white and light green parts**
**¼ cup toasted sesame seeds**
**1 teaspoon dried red pepper flakes**

## GRILL
Follow the recipe for Super-Basic Grilled Eggplant (opposite) but about 30 seconds before the eggplant comes off the grill, brush it with:

**⅓ cup hoisin sauce**

 TOP

When the eggplant comes off the grill, put it on a large platter and sprinkle the eggplant with the scallion mixture.

# GRILLED EGGPLANT with FETA and MARAS PEPPER

EGGPLANT IS huge in Middle Eastern cuisines, so here we combine it with several of our favorite flavors from that part of the world. If you've never used them, Maras peppers and pomegranate molasses are both well worth searching out.

## PREP

While the fire heats up, place in a medium bowl and toss gently to combine:

**1 cup crumbled feta**
**3 tablespoons extra-virgin olive oil**
**2 tablespoons chopped fresh thyme**

## GRILL

Follow the recipe for Super-Basic Grilled Eggplant (see page 200), but about 30 seconds before the eggplant planks come off of the grill, brush them with:

**¼ cup pomegranate molasses, or 2 tablespoons regular molasses mixed with 2 tablespoons fresh lime juice (from 1 lime)**

 **TOP**

When the eggplant comes off the grill, put it on a platter and sprinkle evenly with the feta mixture, then sprinkle it with:

**1 tablespoon Maras pepper flakes**

# MEDITERRANEAN-STYLE GRILLED EGGPLANT RELISH

THIS IS a great condiment with any grilled meats, or you can also serve it with crackers as a kind of dip. It is good both hot and cold and will keep, covered and refrigerated, for about a week. That's what we call versatile.

 **PREP**

While the fire heats up, combine in a large bowl and mix well:

3 tablespoons extra-virgin olive oil

1 tablespoon minced garlic

1 tablespoon capers

1/4 cup roughly chopped pitted black olives

1/2 cup canned tomatoes, diced small

2 tablespoons red wine vinegar

1 teaspoon sugar

2 tablespoons chopped fresh marjoram, thyme, or oregano

Kosher salt and freshly cracked black pepper to taste

 **GRILL**

Follow the recipe for Super-Basic Grilled Eggplant on page 200.

 **TOSS**

When the eggplant comes off the grill, let it cool enough to handle without burning yourself, then dice into medium-size cubes. Put them into the bowl with everything else and toss wildly.

# corn

## Super-Basic
## GRILLED CORN
### 206

## with **Sour Cream, Tabasco,** and **Lime**
### 207

## with **Basil** and **Parmesan**
### 208

## with **Chile Mayo**
### 210

# Super-Basic GRILLED CORN

6 ears of corn, shucked, silks removed, broken in half, and blanched in
boiling water for 2 minutes
3 tablespoons olive oil
Kosher salt and freshly cracked black pepper to taste

 Build a two-level fire in your grill, which means you put all the coals on one side of the grill and leave the other side free of coals. When the flames have died down, all the coals are covered with gray ash, and the temperature is medium (you can hold your hand 6 inches above the grill for 4 to 5 seconds), you're ready to cook.

 Rub the corn ears all over with the oil and sprinkle them with the salt and pepper. Put the ears on the grill directly over the coals and cook, rolling them around to ensure all of the sides are getting some attention from the fire, until they are golden brown all over, which should take 4 to 6 minutes. Remove the corn from the grill, place the ears in a large bowl (along with some butter if you like) and serve.

| Serves 4 to 6 as a side dish |

# GRILLED CORN with SOUR CREAM, TABASCO, and LIME

*THIS ONE'S got it all—richness from the sour cream, heat from the Tabasco, the sharp citrus tang of lime, plus a little earthiness from the cumin.*

**PREP**
While the fire heats up, get these ingredients ready and set out in small individual containers:

- ½ cup sour cream
- 2 tablespoons Tabasco
- 2 tablespoons fresh lime juice (from 1 lime)
- 2 tablespoons toasted cumin seeds or 1 tablespoon ground cumin
- Kosher salt and freshly cracked black pepper to taste

**GRILL**
Follow the recipe for Super-Basic Grilled Corn, opposite.

 **TOSS**

When the ears come off the grill, put them in a giant bowl, add everything else, and toss with some energy.

# GRILLED CORN with BASIL and PARMESAN

*WITH SUPERFRESH CORN and basil right out of the garden, this dish has the unmistakable flavor of summer—but then we throw in some cheese, because after all, why not get that complexity and richness?*

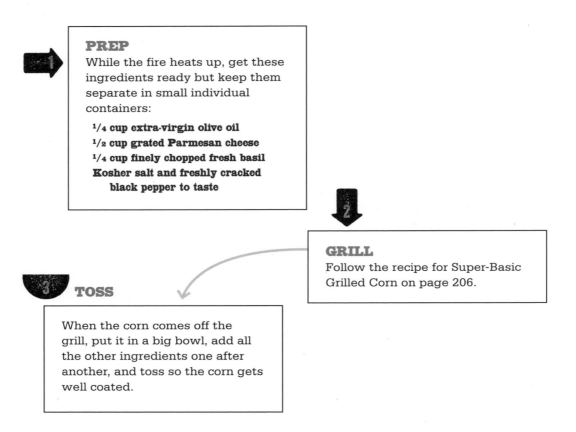

### PREP
While the fire heats up, get these ingredients ready but keep them separate in small individual containers:

¹/₄ cup extra-virgin olive oil
¹/₂ cup grated Parmesan cheese
¹/₄ cup finely chopped fresh basil
Kosher salt and freshly cracked
black pepper to taste

### GRILL
Follow the recipe for Super-Basic Grilled Corn on page 206.

### TOSS
When the corn comes off the grill, put it in a big bowl, add all the other ingredients one after another, and toss so the corn gets well coated.

# GRILLED CORN with CHILE MAYO

*THIS IS inspired by elote, the Mexican-style sweet corn that you can get in the streets of Mexico or, these days, in restaurants all over America.*

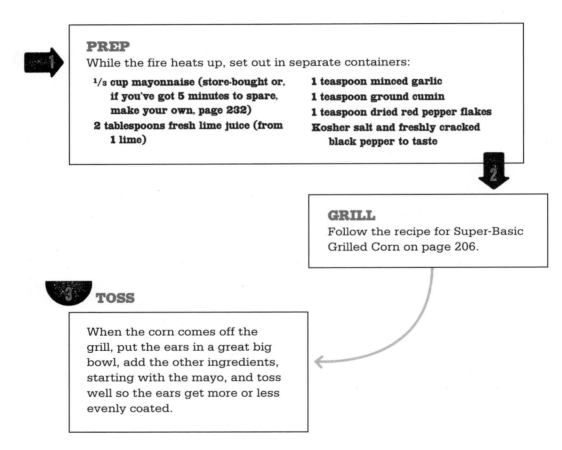

**1**

### PREP
While the fire heats up, set out in separate containers:

- ⅓ cup mayonnaise (store-bought or, if you've got 5 minutes to spare, make your own, page 232)
- 2 tablespoons fresh lime juice (from 1 lime)

- 1 teaspoon minced garlic
- 1 teaspoon ground cumin
- 1 teaspoon dried red pepper flakes
- Kosher salt and freshly cracked black pepper to taste

**2**

### GRILL
Follow the recipe for Super-Basic Grilled Corn on page 206.

**3** TOSS

When the corn comes off the grill, put the ears in a great big bowl, add the other ingredients, starting with the mayo, and toss well so the ears get more or less evenly coated.

# cherry tomatoes

### Super-Basic
## GRILLED CHERRY TOMATOES
212

with **Feta** and **Green Olives**
213

with **Curry, Raisins,** and **Yogurt**
214

with **Fresh Mozzarella, Basil,** and **Pine Nuts**
215

# Super-Basic
# GRILLED CHERRY TOMATOES

1 pint cherry tomatoes, washed and stemmed

3 tablespoons vegetable oil

Kosher salt and freshly cracked black pepper to taste

 Build a two-level fire in your grill, which means you put all the coals on one side of the grill and leave the other side free of coals. When the flames have died down, all the coals are covered with gray ash, and the temperature is medium (you can hold your hand 6 inches above the grill for 4 to 5 seconds), you're ready to cook.

 Toss the cherry tomatoes with the oil and sprinkle them generously with the salt and pepper. Thread onto skewers loosely enough so they are just touching, place the skewers on the grill directly over the coals, and cook, rolling around a few times, just until they are slightly soft and a bit blistered, 3 to 4 minutes. Slide the tomatoes off the skewers and serve.

**Serves 4 as a side dish**

# GRILLED CHERRY TOMATOES with FETA and GREEN OLIVES

*THIS IS really more of a feta salad with cherry tomatoes, but the smokiness of the grilled tomatoes takes it to a new level.*

### PREP
While the fire heats up, set out in separate containers:

²/₃ **cup crumbled feta**
¹/₂ **cup pitted green olives**
**2 tablespoons extra-virgin olive oil**
**1 tablespoon roughly chopped fresh oregano**

### GRILL
Follow the recipe for Super-Basic Grilled Cherry Tomatoes, opposite.

 ### TOSS

When the cherry tomatoes come off the grill, slide them off the skewers into a large bowl, add the other ingredients one after another, and give it all a couple of good tosses.

# GRILLED CHERRY TOMATOES with CURRY, RAISINS, and YOGURT

*HERE YOU HAVE what's basically a grilled tomato chutney. You can eat it on its own as a small side dish, or serve it alongside any grilled chicken dish.*

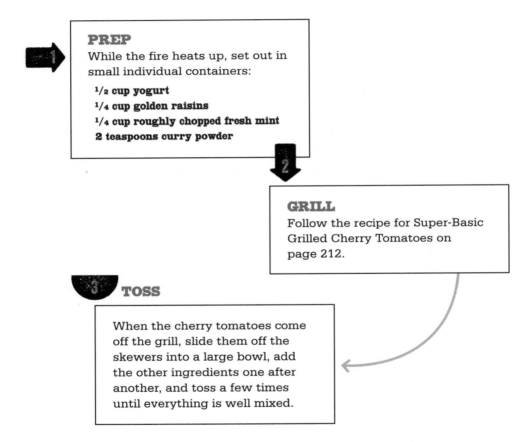

**PREP**

While the fire heats up, set out in small individual containers:

1/2 cup yogurt
1/4 cup golden raisins
1/4 cup roughly chopped fresh mint
2 teaspoons curry powder

**GRILL**

Follow the recipe for Super-Basic Grilled Cherry Tomatoes on page 212.

**TOSS**

When the cherry tomatoes come off the grill, slide them off the skewers into a large bowl, add the other ingredients one after another, and toss a few times until everything is well mixed.

# GRILLED CHERRY TOMATOES with
# FRESH MOZZARELLA, BASIL, and PINE NUTS

*WE LIKE TO pile this mixture, which has all those good Italian flavors, on grilled bread, but it's also refreshing on its own.*

### PREP
While the fire heats up, prepare and set out in separate containers:

- **1 cup medium-diced fresh mozzarella (about 4 ounces)**
- **¹/₄ cup toasted pine nuts**
- **¹/₄ cup roughly chopped fresh basil**
- **1 teaspoon minced garlic**
- **3 tablespoons extra-virgin olive oil**

### GRILL
Follow the recipe for Super-Basic Grilled Cherry Tomatoes on page 212.

### TOSS

When the cherry tomatoes come off the grill, slide them off the skewers into a large bowl, add all of the other ingredients, and toss a few times until everything is well mixed.

# asparagus

## Super-Basic
## GRILLED ASPARAGUS

### with **Simple Vinaigrette** and **Hazelnuts**

### with **Orange-Sesame Mayo**

### with **Sweet and Sour Bacon-Balsamic Vinaigrette**

# Super-Basic
# GRILLED ASPARAGUS

**1¹/₂ pounds small to medium asparagus, trimmed, peeled if you want**
**2 tablespoons vegetable oil**
**Kosher salt and freshly cracked black pepper to taste**

 Build a two-level fire in your grill, which means you put all the coals on one side of the grill and leave the other side free of coals. When the flames have died down, all the coals are covered with gray ash, and the temperature is medium (you can hold your hand 6 inches above the grill for 4 to 5 seconds), you're ready to cook.

 Rub the asparagus all over with the oil and sprinkle generously with the salt and pepper. Place the asparagus on the grill directly over the coals, and cook, rolling them around to ensure all the sides are browning, until the spears are golden brown all over, 5 to 7 minutes. Take off the grill and serve the asparagus hot, warm, or at room temperature.

**Serves 4 as a side dish**

# GRILLED ASPARAGUS with SIMPLE VINAIGRETTE and HAZELNUTS

*WE LIKE USING this recipe with the first asparagus of the spring because it highlights the delicate flavor of those early stalks.*

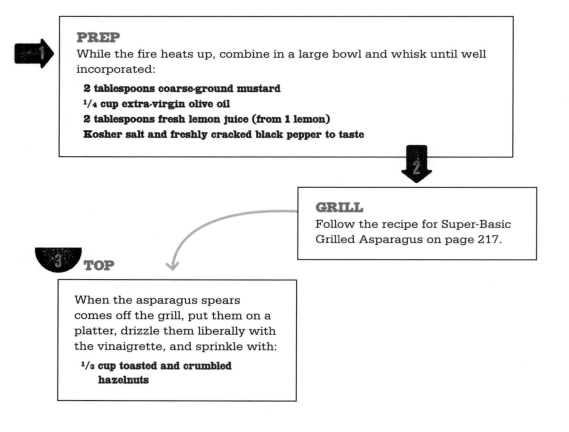

**PREP**
While the fire heats up, combine in a large bowl and whisk until well incorporated:

**2 tablespoons coarse-ground mustard**
**¹/₄ cup extra-virgin olive oil**
**2 tablespoons fresh lemon juice (from 1 lemon)**
**Kosher salt and freshly cracked black pepper to taste**

**GRILL**
Follow the recipe for Super-Basic Grilled Asparagus on page 217.

**TOP**
When the asparagus spears comes off the grill, put them on a platter, drizzle them liberally with the vinaigrette, and sprinkle with:

**¹/₃ cup toasted and crumbled hazelnuts**

# GRILLED ASPARAGUS with ORANGE-SESAME MAYO

*LATER IN THE SEASON, when you've seen a lot of asparagus and want to beef it up with some stronger flavors, this one is for you.*

## PREP

While you're waiting for the fire to heat up and hopefully having a libation of your choice, combine in a large bowl and mix well:

1/2 cup mayo (store-bought is okay, but making your own is easy—page 232)

2 tablespoons fresh orange juice (from 1 orange)

1 teaspoon toasted sesame oil

2 tablespoons soy sauce

1 teaspoon orange zest

1 tablespoon minced fresh ginger

Kosher salt and freshly cracked black pepper to taste

## GRILL

Follow the recipe for Super-Basic Grilled Asparagus on page 217.

 ## TOP

When the asparagus spears come off the grill, put them on a platter, top each with a good smear of the mayo, and serve, passing the rest of the mayo separately for dipping.

*Curve Ball*

# GRILLED ASPARAGUS with SWEET AND SOUR BACON-BALSAMIC VINAIGRETTE

WHEN YOU NEED an excuse to have bacon, this recipe comes in very handy. It still seems refined, in the way that asparagus always does, but it gives you that bacon fix.

### PREP

While the fire heats up, combine in a small bowl:

**⅓ cup balsamic vinegar**
**1 tablespoon sugar**
**1 teaspoon ground coriander**
**Kosher salt and freshly cracked black pepper to taste**

Then cook in a large sauté pan over medium heat until crisp:

**6 slices bacon, diced medium**

Pour off most of the fat, leaving about 2 tablespoons in the pan, and set the bacon aside. When the bacon is cool, crumble it and save it for later.

Return the pan to medium heat and add:

**¼ cup thinly sliced scallions, white and light green parts**

Cook, stirring once in a while, until well softened, 3 to 4 minutes, then add the vinegar mixture. Let this mixture come just to a simmer, then take it off the heat and whisk in:

**2 tablespoons extra-virgin olive oil**

### GRILL

Follow the recipe for Super-Basic Grilled Asparagus on page 217.

 TOP

When the asparagus spears come off the grill, put them on a platter, top with some of the vinaigrette, and sprinkle with the crumbled bacon.

# DRINKS

**GRILLING IS EXCITING**, it's fun, it's relaxing—and, paradoxically, it can be slightly stressful, too. After all, cooking over live fire is kind of the high-wire act of cooking. Each fire is different, and you always run the chance of ruining dinner. It doesn't happen often, but it does occur every once in a while. (If you ever run into Chris, ask him about the time he incinerated a whole pig at a wine and food festival.) We think this is part and parcel of the fun of this supremely interactive cooking method, but it has inspired us to give two pieces of advice to any griller who will listen. First, always keep the phone number of your favorite delivery guy handy, just in case. That way, you'll still be able to feed everyone, and as a bonus, you'll have stories to tell of that time you accidentally torched dinner and had to call for pizza (or falafel or whatever). Second, always have a sufficient supply of your favorite beverage ready to hand out. Not only will it deepen the general convivial atmosphere, but it will also help you relax and enjoy the exciting challenge of grilling rather than stressing over it. Ordinarily, we like to have a good amount of cold beer and chilled wine around. But sometimes you want to step it up and provide your guests (and yourself) with some more elaborate options. And that means cocktails. Fortunately, Chris's nephew, Tom Schlesinger-Guidelli, who is also in the restaurant business, is a charter member of the new generation of cocktail creators. At the inception of the new cocktail movement, they called themselves "mixologists," though "bartenders" now seems to be making a comeback. But in any case, these mixers and shakers have brought a new level of creativity to the once-staid world of cocktails. Tom agreed to create a few recipes for us, following the same format of using one ingredient for several recipes that increase slightly in difficulty as you go along. Each recipe makes one drink, but of course you can multiply the recipe ingredients as many times as you want. You will need a double jigger to measure ingredients for these drinks, and a cocktail shaker and strainer are good ideas, too. Oh, and you'll probably want a muddler. As for the ingredients themselves, Tom often specifies certain brands of booze and bitters, but you should feel free to use whatever you like or have on hand. As he says, "The fun is to play around with alternatives and options and see what works best for you." And this is one place where testing the recipes over and over again somehow doesn't seem to be a problem.

# DRINKS WITH MINT

## MOJITO

*MOST PEOPLE tend to make this classic cocktail, which is intended to focus on the taste of lime and sugarcane, either too sweet or too rum heavy. So Tom added a good dose of lime peel, which not only intensifies the lime, but also adds a pleasant edge of bitter to the drink's flavor profile.*

Combine in a highball glass and *muddle*—in other words, mush them together thoroughly with a muddler or the back of a wooden spoon or something like that:

**Peel of 1 whole lime**
**20 whole mint leaves**
**1 ounce fresh lime juice (from 2 limes)**
**1 ounce Simple Syrup (page 233)**

Once it's all nicely muddled, add:

**1½ ounces white rum**
**Ice to almost fill the glass**

Shake it gently, then top it off with:

**2 ounces soda water**

Garnish with:

**1 sprig mint**

## MINT COBBLER

*THE INTENTION HERE is to use whatever fruit is at the height of its season, so any summer berry will work. You could even use pineapple. Or mango. You get the idea.*

Combine in a highball glass and muddle:

**10 fresh blueberries, raspberries, blackberries, or strawberries**
**10 whole mint leaves**
**¾ ounce fresh lime juice (from 1 lime)**
**¾ ounce Simple Syrup (recipe page 233)**

Now add:

**2 ounces brandy**
**Ice to fill the glass**

Pass back and forth gently between two glasses to mix.
Garnish with:

**1 sprig mint**

# MINT FREEZE

*EVERYBODY LOVES a frozen drink in hot weather, so here's our contribution. The mint-ginger simple syrup gives you the option to play around, adding spices like cardamom or cinnamon without altering the texture of the drink. We recommend using crushed ice here because it blends more quickly, so it introduces less heat*

Combine in a blender and blend for 10 seconds, or until ice is fully incorporated:

**1 ounce white rum**

**1 ounce dark rum (like Old Monk, Myers, or Goslings)**

**1/2 ounce fresh lime juice (from 1 lime)**

**1/2 ounce fresh orange juice (from 1 orange)**

**1 ounce Mint-Ginger Simple Syrup (recipe below)**

**3 dashes Angostura Bitters**

**1 1/2 cups crushed ice**

Garnish with:

**1 sprig mint**

**Freshly grated nutmeg**

# MINT-GINGER SIMPLE SYRUP

Make a batch of Simple Syrup (page 233), but for every 1 cup of sugar, add about 1/2 cup of mint leaves and a tablespoon or so of minced ginger before you put the mixture over the heat. This makes a lot, but in addition to making this cocktail, you can mix it with sparkling water for a refreshing nonalcoholic summer drink. And feel free to add a touch of cinnamon, cardamom, nutmeg, or any other warm spice to jazz it up a bit more.

# DRINKS WITH GINGER

## HOUSE GINGER BEER

*THIS IS THE BASIS for all of our ginger drinks, plus it makes an awesome summer drink all by itself. If you like superspicy, you can double the amount of Atomic Chile Water (recipe below). The bitters that we call for make a very complex and interesting drink, but you can substitute any other bitters you fancy, or just use all regular Angostura if that's what you've got on hand. If you don't have a juicer, just coarsely grate the peeled knob of ginger, then squeeze it in cheesecloth to extract the juice.*

Combine in a pitcher or other glass container:

**3 ounces ginger juice, from a knob of ginger about 4 inches long**

**5 ounces Simple Syrup (page 233)**

**4 ounces fresh lemon juice (from 1 to 2 lemons)**

**1½ ounces Atomic Chile Water (recipe below)**

**16 ounces cold water**

**7 dashes Angostura Orange Bitters**

**2 dashes Angostura Bitters**

*IF YOU HAVE A SODA SIPHON:* **Make sure the siphon is cold and add all the ingredients. Then add one soda charge. Remove the charge, shake the siphon, and then refrigerate for at least an hour before you use it.**

*IF YOU DON'T HAVE A SODA SIPHON:* **Add ½ cup soda water, stir gently, then refrigerate for at least an hour before serving.**

## ATOMIC CHILE WATER

In a food processor or blender, puree:

**2 Thai chiles, stemmed but not seeded**

**1 teaspoon minced fresh ginger**

**5 tablespoons water**

**1½ teaspoons white vinegar**

**Pinch of kosher salt**

Add:

**¾ cup boiling water**

Pour into a glass or heat-resistant plastic container, cover, and let sit at room temperature for a couple of days before using.

# DARK AND STORMY

CHRIS IS so fond of this drink that he named his boat after it. It's a classic, and—once you've got your House Ginger Beer in the fridge—it could not possibly be easier.

Pour into a highball glass over ice:

**4 ounces House Ginger Beer (page 227, or you can use any superspicy commercial ginger beer such as Goya)**

Pour on top:

**2 ounces Old Monk or other dark rum**

Garnish with:

**Lime wedge**

# BOHEMIAN COOLER

ST. GERMAIN is a perfect example of a product that went from "What the heck is it?" to bartender's favorite in what seemed like a few weeks. This easy summer highball gets a lot of complexity from the elegant floral sweetness of St. Germain.

Pour into a highball glass over ice and stir well:

**1½ ounces St. Germain Elderflower Liqueur**

**¾ ounce Rittenhouse Rye Whiskey**

**¾ ounce fresh lemon juice (from 1 lemon)**

Top with House Ginger Beer (page 227; or you can use any superspicy commercial ginger beer such as Goya)

# DRINKS WITH PINEAPPLE

## PIÑA COLADA

DILUTING the coconut cream with heavy cream makes this tropical classic somewhat less sweet and more balanced than the versions you're likely to find in vacation hotels in the Caribbean.

Combine in a highball glass:

**2 ounces Plantation 5-year-old rum or other amber rum**

**1/3 ounce coconut cream**

**2/3 ounce heavy cream**

**1 ounce canned or boxed pineapple juice**

Add ice to fill the glass and stir well.

## KING CAESAR

THIS DRINK, named after a boating magnate from Duxbury, Massachusetts (yes, his name really is King Caesar), is a perfect poolside drink, and also batches up really well as a punch for a crowd. You can multiply it by 10, make it in advance, and then add a bottle of Cava and some ice just before serving. Amaro is one of a class of potable bitters such as Campari, but with more tropical spice than that more familiar brand.

Combine in a mixing glass:

**3/4 ounce fresh lime juice (from 1 lime)**

**3/4 ounce canned or boxed pineapple juice**

**3/4 ounce Amaro Montenegro**

**1/2 ounce Demerara Syrup (Simple Syrup, page 233, made with Demerara sugar)**

**1 dash of Tiki Bitters**

Add ice, shake well, then pour through a tea strainer into a flute and top with:

**2 ounces Cava**

# THREADNEEDLE

THIS IS more of a serious drinker's cocktail, in the Manhattan/martini mode. At Island Creek Oyster Bar, Tom infuses brandy with juniper branches, then uses just that brandy in this drink; he's added the gin here so you can get the right juniper flavor without having to go that far. Pimm's Cup reinforces the juniper characteristic, so the drink is named after the street in London where it is said that distinctive liquor was first made.

Combine in a mixing glass:

**1 1/2 ounces Pimm's Cup**
**1/2 ounce brandy**
**1/2 ounce gin**
**1/2 ounce Pineapple Syrup (recipe below)**
**1 dash of Regan's Orange Bitters or other orange bitters**

Stir well, then strain into a chilled rocks glass. Garnish with:

**Twist of lemon**

# PINEAPPLE SYRUP

THIS RECIPE makes a lot: you can use half or a quarter of a pineapple and decrease the other ingredients by the same amount, but the syrup is very delicious combined with sparkling water and a little lime juice, so why not make a big batch?

Peel and slice into rounds:

**1 whole ripe pineapple**

Combine in a large saucepan:

**8 cups sugar**
**4 cups water**

Bring to a boil, then stir until the sugar is completely dissolved.

Add the pineapple, then cover and refrigerate for 12 hours. Blend in a mixer and pass through fine chinois or a tea strainer.

Add:

**Kosher salt to taste**

Bottle and refrigerate. This will keep for about 2 weeks.

# a few small component recipes

THERE ARE A HANDFUL of ingredients in our recipes that you can either buy at the store or make yourself, but that we think are worth making at home. They're easy enough if you have a few minutes to spare, plus they taste better. So here they are.

## HOMEMADE MAYONNAISE

Makes about 1¼ cups

1 egg yolk

2 teaspoons coarse-ground mustard

Kosher salt and freshly cracked black pepper to taste

2 teaspoons fresh lemon juice (from 1 lemon)

1 cup vegetable oil of your choice

*FOOD PROCESSOR METHOD:* Combine the egg yolk, mustard, salt, pepper, and lemon juice in a food processor and turn on the motor. While the motor is running, add the oil in a slow, steady stream. (Most newer food processors have a little hole in the feed-tube insert, so you just have to pour the oil into the insert.) When it looks like mayonnaise, stop the machine, taste, and add more salt and pepper if needed.

*BLENDER METHOD:* Follow the same procedure as for the food processor method above. Put on the lid of the blender before you turn it on, then take out the insert in the lid and drizzle the oil in through that.

*IMMERSION BLENDER METHOD:* Combine everything but the oil in the immersion blender cup or some other tall, narrow container that's just big enough so the business end of the immersion blender will go down to the bottom. (An aluminum cocktail shaker is a good option.) Gently pour in the oil, then wait 5 minutes or so for the oil to (mostly) rise to the top. Put the blender down at the bottom of the container, turn it on, tilt it very slightly, and slowly draw it up to the top. By the time you get to the top, you'll have mayonnaise.

# HOMEMADE SUN-DRIED (OKAY, OVEN-DRIED) TOMATOES

32 tomato halves

  16 plum tomatoes
  1/4 cup extra-virgin olive oil
  Kosher salt and freshly cracked black pepper
    to taste
  2 tablespoons minced fresh rosemary
    (optional)
  2 teaspoons ground cumin (optional)

Preheat the oven to 200°F. Trim the stem end of the tomatoes, split them in half lengthwise, drizzle them with the oil, and sprinkle them with the salt and pepper, rosemary, and/or cumin. Place the tomatoes skin side down in a single layer on a drying rack set on top of a sheet pan and put it in the oven for about 8 hours. (This is a good thing to do at night while you're sleeping.) The tomatoes should be reduced in size by about one-quarter, shriveled up on the outside, but still tender and juicy on the inside. They can be stored, covered and refrigerated, for 4 or 5 days.

# HOMEMADE ROASTED RED PEPPERS

Makes as many red bell peppers as you have

Light a fire in your grill; when the fire is medium-hot (you can hold your hand 6 inches above the grill grid for about 3 to 4 seconds), put the peppers on the grill directly over the fire. Grill the peppers, moving them around with your tongs, until all sides are uniformly black and charred. Remove them from the grill and place in a paper bag or in a bowl covered with plastic wrap for 20 minutes to loosen the skins. Peel off the charred skins, remove the stems, seeds, and ribs, and use right away or cover with plastic wrap and refrigerate for up to 2 weeks.

# SIMPLE SYRUP

Makes 1/2 cup

  1/2 cup water
  1/2 cup sugar

Bring the water to a boil over high heat, then pour in the sugar, stirring as you do. When the sugar is fully dissolved, you have simple syrup. Let it cool and use it in all kinds of cocktails. (See, wasn't that simple?)

# ingredients

THERE ARE some ingredients we use in this book that may be unfamiliar to you, so we thought we'd explain what they are and why we like them.

### Cardamom

To us, cardamom is the very definition of exotic flavors; just a pinch of it can transform all kinds of dishes. This spice, which is related to ginger, comes in both green and black, though green is much more common. Either one can be used ground or in whole pods, but it makes most sense to buy it in whole pods and then grind it yourself, either in a mortar and pestle or an electric spice grinder, since it loses its strong aromatics and sweet herbal flavors quickly after it's ground. You can either extract the seeds from the pods and grind them, or you can grind the pods whole, as long as you grind them very fine.

### Chile Sambal

Chile sambal is a classic condiment from Southeast Asia made from ground spicy chile peppers. There are many options available, some with garlic (chile-garlic Ssambal), others with fish sauce, shrimp paste, or vinegar. All of them have a bright red color from the fresh chiles and can really pack a punch, depending on the desired amount of heat for the dish.

### Chipotles in Adobo

Once relatively rare, chipotles in adobo (or en adobo) are now easily found in the canned section of the grocery store. That's a very good thing, because the smoky heat of chipotles is pretty much an ideal partner for grilled foods.

"In adobo" (or "en adobo") simply means that the chiles are combined with a deep red, vinegary tomato sauce. You can buy chipotles in dried form, too, but en adobo is our favorite way to use these guys, because the sauce adds an extra bit of flavor, plus you don't need to worry about reconstituting them as you would with dried ones.

### Gochugaru

A staple ingredient in kimchi, *gochugaru* is basically dried red peppers coarsely ground down so they have a texture somewhere between flakes and powder. *Gochugaru* is spicy-hot, but it also has some sweetness to it and a bit of smoke, as well. The tastiest versions are made from sun-dried chiles, and they are also the most expensive, of course.

### Maras Pepper

Along with Urfa this is one of the dried flaked chile peppers that are ubiquitous in Turkey. This cherry-red pepper has a bright flavor, brash and fruity but with a very faint edge of bitterness, and its complex initial taste is followed by a mild, slow-building heat. Like its cousin Urfa, it has a wide variety of uses, from vinaigrettes to stews to spice rubs. These two chiles have become Doc's favorite spices—he tends to sprinkle them into or onto everything, and he once took a trip to the towns in southern Turkey where they are produced, just to understand them better. If you take his advice, you'll follow the Turks' example and just leave these out on your table ready at hand.

### Mirin

Mirin is a sweet rice wine that's pretty much indispensable in Japanese cooking. It is normally golden in color with a thick consistency and a sweet taste. It is classically used with seafood, but we think it's also a good match with pork.

### Scotch Bonnet Peppers

You know how people say that an ingredient "changed their life"? Well, Scotch bonnets did kind of change Chris's life. When he discovered them on a surfing trip to Barbados back in the 1970s, their extreme heat, backed up by a distinctive floral flavor, was a revelation. They confirmed his feeling that hot, spicy food was the culinary road for him, and inspired him to create a range of popular dishes and make and bottle Inner Beauty Hot Sauce. Later they led to the extraordinarily popular Hell Nights at his restaurant, the East Coast Grill. They have since been eclipsed in capsaicin count, but Scotch Bonnets were once the world's hottest known peppers—and they do pack a real wallop. Found mostly in the Caribbean, they are most familiar as an essential ingredient in genuine jerk sauce.

### Seaweeds: Nori, Wakame, and Kombu

**NORI:** Nori is a popular type of dried seaweed used to make different types of sushi in Japanese cuisine and now readily available in the United States as dried sheets or rolls. It can be used as a crumbled topping, as a wrap for sushi, or rehydrated for a cold salad. However used, it provides a salty, faintly herbal flavor.

**WAKAME:** Wakame is another type of edible seaweed that can be used dry or, more commonly, rehydrated in a soup or salad. It is perhaps the purest representation of the fifth taste, called umami, which is most easily translated as "savoriness."

**KOMBU:** Kombu is a type of edible kelp often used in Japan to make soup stock. It can be eaten dried, sprinkled as a condiment, or rehydrated as a salad as is popular in American sushi restaurants. It has a mild, salty flavor that is maybe best described as "green."

### Shichimi Togarashi Powder

Also known as seven-spice powder, shichimi togarashi is a popular Japanese condiment made from a variety of ingredients, including ground chile peppers, dried citrus peel, seaweed, and ginger. With its vivid red-orange color and smoky, citrusy, briny flavor, it can be sprinkled on noodles, soups, or salads, rubbed on meats, or added to sauces to enhance complexity without too much heat. It's a really nice one to have in the pantry.

### Smoked Paprika

While plain old paprika is simply ground dried paprika, a mild chile pepper, smoked paprika adds an extra layer of flavor since the chile peppers are smoked before processing. The best versions, called *Pimentón de la Vera*, are produced in the La Vera Valley of northern Spain, where the peppers are smoked in the traditional way over open wood fires. *Pimentón* comes in three varieties: sweet, bittersweet, and hot; we like the bittersweet, because it's most versatile. But even if you buy the less upscal, smoked paprika they have in the grocery stores, it's a quick and easy way to add smokiness and a hint of heat to a wide range of dishes. It also makes a very nice spice rub for pork all by itself.

### Sriracha

Think of Sriracha as the new ketchup. It is a vinegary hot sauce from Thailand that has become wildly popular in restaurants and at home. It has a bright red color and is made from chile peppers, vinegar, garlic, and spices, so it can pack some heat. Put it out on the table and use it on and in everything.

### Sumac

Sumac, the ground dried berry of the sumac tree, has a tart, citruslike flavor. It is widely used in cuisines of the Eastern Mediterranean and Middle East. This is partially because sour flavors are more valued in those regions than in Euro-derived cuisines, and partially because it grows there and provides a quick and convenient way to brighten up the flavors of sauces, grilled meats, salads, fish—basically any dish in which you might use lemon. The nice thing about using sumac instead of lemon, though, is that sumac is less aggressive, with a subtler, milder tartness. Plus it doesn't go bad.

### Szechuan Peppercorns

Szechuan peppercorns are used throughout Asia, especially in the Sichuan province of China, and are one of the main ingredients in Chinese five-spice powder. Despite their name, they are not peppercorns at all but the dried husks of a type of citrus plant, which can be used whole or ground. They have a distinctive pink color with a citrusy, slightly vegetal flavor, and the unique quality of imparting a tongue-numbing sensation when used in sufficient quantities.

### Toasted Sesame Oil

Prevalent in Asian and Middle Eastern cuisines, toasted sesame oil is used as a flavoring agent. In that, it differs from the untoasted oil, which is more often used as a cooking medium, as Americans use vegetable oil. It's easy to tell the two apart, since the toasted oil is brown, while the untoasted is light yellow. As with all nuts and seeds, toasting gives the sesame seeds— and the oil pressed from them—a richer, very distinctly nutty flavor.

### Urfa Pepper

This is one of two dried flaked chile peppers (the other is Maras) that are routinely set out on the tables of every café and kebab joint in Turkey. This pepper, which is fermented, is a deep oxblood red, with a mild heat and an earthy, smoky flavor that contains an echo of tobacco. We recommend you use it widely.

### Wasabi Powder

Real wasabi, also known as Japanese horseradish, comes from the root of the plant *Wasabia japonica*. It has an intense spicy green herbal flavor, and is an excellent alternative to the more usual chile peppers as a source of heat. Wasabi powder is a simple and less expensive alternative to the fresh variety, and when mixed with water to form a paste can be used to add flavor to raw and cooked fish, noodles, dips, dressings, and more. Be warned, though, that the cheaper versions of this powder often contain no actual *Wasabia japonica*, but instead are made up of mustard powder, powdered regular horseradish, and spinach powder for coloring, so pay attention to the labels.

# index

Ten Speed Press and the Ten Speed Press colophon
are registered trademarks of Random House LLC

Library of Congress Cataloging-in-Publication Data
on file with the publisher

Hardcover ISBN: 978-1-60774-527-3
eBook ISBN: 978-1-60774-528-0

Printed in China

Design by Toni Tajima
Food stylist: George Dolese
Food styling assistant: Nan Bullock
Prop stylist: Ethel Brennan

10 9 8 7 6 5 4 3 2 1

First Edition